They Wrote on Clay

58

They Wrote on Clay

The Babylonian Tablets
Speak Today

By

EDWARD CHIERA

Edited by

GEORGE G. CAMERON

THE UNIVERSITY OF CHICAGO PRESS

THE UNIVERSITY OF CHICAGO PRESS, CHICAGO 60637
The University of Chicago Press, Ltd., London W. C. 1

4156

Preface

ONE day Professor Chiera was guiding some visitors through the exhibition halls of the Oriental Institute of the University of Chicago. They stopped first in front of the huge Assyrian bull or "cherub," which he himself had found and brought to this country, then passed through the Assyrian Hall containing the massive stone reliefs from the palace of Sargon of Assyria. As they turned to enter the room containing the ancient clay tablets and records, one of the members of the party chanced to remark, "Now that we've seen the most interesting things, let's rush through here as quickly as possible."

That was so typical of the average attitude toward Babylonian-Assyrian discoveries that Professor Chiera, stopping short, said, "Wait a minute! The real interest starts here," and proceeded to discuss some of the important information that we may secure from these ancient "books of clay." This volume is an enlargement of the talk he gave there.

It is not difficult to explain this attitude on the part of the visitor to the museum, for there is a glamour, an irresistible fascination, about magnificent gold objects from Ur of the Chaldees, exquisitely carved ivories from Megiddo or Armageddon, or stupendous reliefs from ancient Persepolis. We forget so easily that these, and the minor finds of archeology, could tell but half a tale without the inscriptions; that they and the texts on clay, stone, and parchment are mutually complementary; that the one interprets the other and is incomplete without the other.

Yet the lure of these more obvious archeological finds is only partly the cause of the comparative obscurity under which the records of the past labor. We, who pride ourselves on being "Assyriologists," are to blame also. We have lost touch with the public because we have been unable to see beyond our own noses. We have been so wrapped up in our linguistic and historical "research" that only recently has it begun to dawn upon us that if the results we have attained are interesting to us they would also be of interest to the intelligent man engaged in other lines of endeavor. Gradually we are becoming aware that outsiders would like to know what relationship Assyriology can possibly have to their own lives.

Our previous lack of contact outside the field is due likewise to our youth. It is but a hundred years since an intrepid adventurer clambered up the face of a perilous rock to secure for us the means wherewith our science might advance. So young are we that our very terminology is inept. Few there are indeed who know that the name of our science, "Assyriology," is based on an accident—the fact that the first large group of texts ever discovered was written in Assyrian. Few are aware that Assyrian itself is but one dialect, Babylonian another, of a language which is called, in our esoteric circles, "Akkadian."

But however remote the activities of Assyriologists may

have seemed to the public in the past, today the workers in this field are keen to bring home to the layman the significance of their labors. And Professor Chiera, through his combination of brilliant scholarship and gift of felicitous presentation of his subject, was especially well adapted to render this service. It is, therefore, regrettable that his untimely death prevented him from realizing his dream of sharing with the public at large his interest in and knowledge of the fascinating records of men who lived millenniums ago.

Fortunately, before his last illness he had written the first draft of a book intended for this purpose. Friends urged its posthumous publication, and at the request of Mrs. Chiera I have prepared this edition. In it I have endeavored to retain as far as possible Professor Chiera's style and method of presentation. We may be sure that the talk he gave that day in the museum halls was well received; let us hope that this edition of the book which he left unfinished will meet with a similar reception.

GEORGE G. CAMERON

CHICAGO, ILLINOIS
January 3, 1938

Table of Contents

PROLOGUE xi
1. THE TREASURE HUNT 1
2. BOOKS EVERLASTING 17
3. THE MOUND OF SEVEN CITIES 23
4. THE DAWN OF UNDERSTANDING 40
5. ANCIENT ABC's 50
6. THE WORLD OF BUSINESS 67
7. THE BUSINESS OF RELIGION 80
8. KINGS' TALES 90
9. PRIESTS' TALES 106
10. BABEL AND BIBLE 118
11. THE SEARCH FOR TRUTH 135
12. THE PHILOSOPHER'S STONE 147
13. THE THREE R's 165
14. A PEOPLE'S RESURRECTION 176
15. ARTS AND THE MAN 192
16. LEAVES FROM A DIPLOMAT'S DIARY 201
17. ON TO GREECE AND ROME 212
18. WEST AND EAST 222
EPILOGUE 231
ACKNOWLEDGMENTS 234

Prologue

From a Letter of the Author to His Wife

This evening I made my usual pilgrimage to the mound covering the ancient temple tower. It is only a few hundred yards from our camp, and it is pleasant to ascend to the summit of that tower, which dominates the landscape. This I generally do in the evening, after supper, in the bright moonlight. Today I have come with the ambition of jotting down my impressions, for the spectacle moves me deeply.

Seen from below, it does not look so high as might be expected of a Babylonian temple tower. Did not that of Babylon pretend to reach to heaven? One gets the answer after ascending it. Though rather low (it can hardly be more than five hundred feet), still from the top the eye sweeps over an enormous distance on the boundless, flat plain. Nothing breaks the view, and the plain finally melts into the horizon. About twenty miles away rises the high mound of Cutha. This city was sacred to Nergal, the god of pestilence and of the underworld. The ruins of Babylon are nearer. All around the tower small heaps of dirt represent all that remains of Kish, one of the oldest cities of Mesopotamia.

On all sides is desert. The yellowish soil is arid and thirsty, and no plant can survive the parching heat of the summer; sheep and camels must feed on whatever remains of the grass that has managed to sprout in the few weeks after the rains. The large network of canals, which in ancient times distributed the waters of the Euphrates over all this land, is now represented by a series of small mounds of dirt, running in all directions. Even the Euphrates has abandoned this land by changing its course. In ancient times it came very near to the city, giving water in abundance and affording an easy way of communication.

But man has not yet forsaken this place and still tries to wrest something from the avaricious ground. A mile away an Arab peasant, chanting a plaintive song, is urging on two skinny donkeys that pull a primitive plow. He is placing his trust in the coming rains, hoping these may help multiply the few grains of barley that he will throw into the shallow furrow. If the rains should fail, so will the bread in his house. He works without energy, and the plow wriggles uncertainly over the plain.

Immediately before me, and all around the tower, are the deep trenches made during last year's excavation. It is getting darker, and they are not well defined. But at night, with a full moon, they appear pitch black and bottomless—a line of defense around the sacred mountain, ready to swallow whoever should attempt to approach it. The sun has just now disappeared, and a purple sky smiles, unmindful of this scene of desolation. The cool evening breeze attempts to tear away from my hand the sheet of paper on which I write these notes.

A dead city! I have visited Pompeii and Ostia, and I have taken walks along the empty corridors of the Palatine. But those cities are not dead: they are only temporarily abandoned. The hum of life is still heard, and life blooms all around. They are but a step in the progress of that civilization to which they have contributed their full share and which marches on, under their very eyes.

Here only is real death. Not a column or an arch still stands to demonstrate the permanency of human work. Everything has crumbled into dust. The very temple tower, the most imposing of all these ancient constructions, has entirely lost its original shape. Where are now its seven stages? Where the large stairway that led to the top? Where the shrine that crowned it? We see nothing but a mound of earth—all that remains of the millions of its bricks. On the very top some traces of walls. But these are shapeless: time and neglect have completed their work.

Under my feet are some holes which have been burrowed by foxes and jackals. At night they descend stealthily from their haunts in their difficult search for food, and appear silhouetted against the sky. This evening they appear to sense my presence and stay in hiding, perhaps wondering at this stranger who has come to disturb their peace. The mound is covered with white bones which represent the accumulated evidence of their hunts.

It is beginning to be really dark, and the plaintive song of the Arab has ceased. Nothing breaks the deathly silence. Cutha and Babylon have been swallowed by the darkness. In the distance some lights appear, and I can distinguish those of a village of "friendly" Arabs who are employed in the excavation. Farther away is an encampment of Beduins, here considered as enemies. To us they represent an element of danger, for they are born thieves. But I who have accepted their hospitality and drunk their coffee, made with dirty water and served in cups that are never washed, cannot call them enemies. They have been so trusting that they even let me take some photographs of them, a favor rarely obtained from the Beduins of the desert: who knows what danger might threaten if these should be used in black magic? They are friends, therefore, in so far as they can be friends of a foreigner and unbeliever.

A jackal is now sending forth his howl, half-cry and half-threat. All the dogs of the Arab village immediately take up his challenge, and for a moment the peace is upset by howling and barking.

It is now quite dark. Caution would advise descending immediately to avoid the danger of falling into one of the many trenches. But a certain fascination holds me here. I should like to find a reason for all this desolation. Why should a flourishing city, the seat of an empire, have completely disappeared? Is it the fulfilment of a prophetic curse that changed a superb temple into a den of jackals? Did the actions of the people who lived here have anything to do with this, or is it the fatal destiny of mankind that all its civilizations must crumble when they reach their peak? And what are we doing here, trying to wrest from the past its secrets, when probably we ourselves and our own achievements may become an object of search for peoples to come?

I have to descend now. The moon has not yet risen, and had not my frequent visits taught me the right path to follow, the descent would be really dangerous. Still absorbed in my thoughts

I feel no desire to break up their course by joining my friends. In the semiobscurity I walk toward the open country and the ruins, still untouched, of the ancient city. The ground is soft, being made up entirely of the debris of centuries, and at times my foot sinks in it up to the ankle. Here the ancient habitations, with their mysteries and their tombs, have been sleeping quietly for millenniums. In a few months, perhaps in a few days, here also the ground will be broken by trenches as in a battlefield. And the repose of the poor dead will be disturbed by the frantic search for records and data. . . . .

Chapter 1

THINKING man has always been interested in his past. Archeology, the study of ancient things, has long since helped us to understand more fully our classical background. Within the last century, however, there have appeared those older, and in some ways more brilliant, cultures which preceded Greece and Rome. To some, Egypt represents the center of these earlier cultures, for excavations there have been rewarded by such wonderful discoveries that the very word "archeology" immediately calls to mind the impressive monuments of that land. The famous finds in Tutenkhamon's tomb fired popular imagination to such an extent that for a time our ladies wore Egyptian jewelry and dresses decorated with patterns and scenes copied from the walls of ancient tombs. But even after scarabs and gaudy prints had returned to their former oblivion, something still remained. No one could forget entirely the thousands of pictures which had appeared in books, periodicals, and newspapers. Archeology had won a place in the interest of the masses; and, fortunately for the science, that interest has not abated with the passing years.

But while Tutenkhamon deserves much credit for his help in awakening the world to the importance of our science, yet he has helped to accentuate a tendency that

1

is in itself wrong. The relative importance of archeological results has come to be identified more and more with the intrinsic worth or the artistic value of the objects found. No scholar needs to be told that this is a mistake. The plan of a building, the special pattern or decoration of a lowly clay vessel, a few lines of inscription hardly visible on a rock or a tablet, frequently add much more to scientific knowledge than a hoard of gold or silver objects. As a result of this incorrect evaluation of archeological results some of the most important discoveries made in Egypt have passed unnoticed by the outside world.

Other lands have suffered even more, and this is especially true of that ancient cradle of civilization which is in the basin of the Tigris and Euphrates rivers. If there is a more fertile spot for archeological investigations, it has not yet come to my attention. The "happy hunting ground" for those excavators who desire to see their labors continued even after death is certain to be located there. And yet Mesopotamian archeology does not "make the front page" nearly so often as it deserves. True, the extraordinary finds in the tombs of Ur of the Chaldees have attracted considerable attention. The imposing helmet of solid gold, the splendid filigree work on golden daggers, the unique hair ornaments of Sumerian ladies, and many other objects—all of which testify to a very high degree of civilization dating back as far as 3000 B.C.—have been featured in newspapers and periodicals. More recently, the huge Assyrian "bull" which I was fortunate enough to bring to the Oriental Institute of the University of Chicago from the palace of Sargon in

2

Khorsabad (see illustration opposite title-page) has also received its due share of attention. But here, again, the emphasis was misplaced. The more comments I heard, the more I was convinced that there is widespread ignorance as to the real worth of the results obtainable from Mesopotamian excavations.

A QUEEN OF "UR OF THE CHALDEES" AND HER GOLDEN ORNAMENTS

For this there are three main causes. First, the science of Assyriology is still comparatively young. It takes a long time for new discoveries to escape from the incomprehensible scientific books and articles which first discussed them and to find their place in those general works on history, the arts, and sciences which are easily accessible to all. Moreover, engrossed as they have been in the tasks before them, Assyriologists have either neglected or been unable to present to the world at large in an effective way the importance of the results they have achieved. The last, but by no means least, important reason for this apparent lack of information about our science must be sought in special conditions within the land itself.

With the passing of years the first of these handicaps, the youth of the science, will automatically disappear. Nothing can remain young forever. As time goes on, there will be found a larger number of reliable exponents who can explain lucidly and simply the significance of their efforts. But the last handicap, the one arising from local conditions, is destined to remain forever.

In Egypt stone is plentiful, and the great pharaohs utilized it for temple and pyramid, imperishable testimonies to their names. Even had Egypt's history not been practically continuous, still no one could have failed to notice these reminders of the existence of a great civilization.

In Mesopotamia, on the other hand, stone hardly exists. Some sort of gypsum is found in the north, and this exclusively was used by the Assyrian kings in the decoration of their palaces. But this stone is of such poor quality as to be virtually soluble in water; any inscription or statue left exposed to the elements will promptly disintegrate. In the southern part of the land even gypsum is lacking, and for this reason the ancient Babylonians treasured what pieces of stone they could import from distant lands and used those pieces exclusively for the images of their gods and their most important records. For building materials they had to make the most of what was at at hand, river clay, and the Bible preserves for us a tradition which is based on demonstrable facts:

And it came to pass, as they journeyed from the east, that they found a plain in the land of Shinar; and they dwelt there. And they said one to another, Go to, let us make brick, and burn them thoroughly. And they had brick for stone, and slime had they for mortar [Gen. 11:2–3].

THE WEATHERED STATUE OF AN ASSYRIAN DEITY

MODERN BRICKMAKERS IN THE NEAR EAST

This is correct except that the Babylonians did not always burn their bricks; when they did, they succeeded so well that they obtained a product greatly superior to anything manufactured in that area today. I shall never forget a little episode to which I was witness while visiting the excavations at Ur. One day a guest, a British architect, found in the refuse dump a baked brick dating about 2200 B.C. He wanted to keep it; and, since the inscription stamped upon it was so common as to be of no scientific interest, it was given to him. But the brick was large, about twelve inches square and three inches thick—quite a burden to carry as far as England. Our guest decided it would be wiser to cut off the inscription and take away only that. He borrowed an ax and worked with it over half an hour under the broiling sun, but the brick refused to be cut. He had to give up but, despite his disappointment, could not refrain from expressing his admiration for the wonderful work of the ancient brickmakers.

The early contractor had to meet one difficulty. Fuel was as expensive in the Orient in those times as it is today, and the immense temples and palaces that ancient architects were constantly planning required such an extraordinarily large number of bricks that the cost of baking them would have been prohibitive. So the old Babylonians resorted to the very simple expedient of drying their bricks in the sun and using them unbaked. The

RESTORING A WALL WITH MUD BRICKS

ANCIENT WALL CONSTRUCTION AND DRAINAGE CHANNELS

walls exposed to the elements were protected by plaster of mud and straw, or sometimes with baked bricks set in bitumen. Courtyards were also paved with baked bricks, but the interior of the walls was a solid mass of sun-dried bricks. Building costs were thus cut considerably, and the construction remained solid so long as the roof stood and the facing continued in good condition. But, let the edifice be neglected for a number of years, and it would crumble into dust.

When the central government became too weak or too poor to take proper care of the network of canals that irrigated the land, large tracts of fertile territory were converted into a desert almost overnight, and whole cities had to be abandoned. The roofs of the buildings caved

MODERN WALL CONSTRUCTION

in, and the core of the huge walls, no longer protected, was exposed to the rain. Water slowly worked in; the bricks began to swell up, and the walls to crack and fall. After a few rainy seasons, the upper part of the walls completely disintegrated and left merely a little mound of dirt to mark the site of a once splendid palace. All furniture and perishable objects that had not been taken away when the buildings were abandoned remained buried in the wet debris; with the passing of years they too disappeared and are now gone forever. We should have no idea of the magnificence of the ancient furnishings but for the fact that occasionally we find thrones, chairs, and tables sculptured on the reliefs which adorned the palaces.

A CRUMBLING MUD-BRICK WALL IN A MODERN NEAR EASTERN CITY

In Egypt conditions were entirely different. The dry climate, the very scanty rainfall, and the fact that the sands would not absorb and hold moisture have all collaborated in favor of the archeologists; bits of papyri buried in the sands have been found in perfect condition after thousands of years. Religion has also played a part in the preservation of remains. The ancient Egyptians surpassed all other peoples in the effort to provide their dead, from the humblest subject to the mightiest pharaoh, with the many conveniences they might need in their future life. Of course, the greater the power and means of an individual, the more thorough were the preparations to assure his happiness after death.

From highest antiquity important Egyptian personages were surrounded in their tombs with their most precious possessions. But trouble soon developed: the rich contents of the tombs attracted robbers. In spite of all precautions—of building the tomb inside a huge pyramid (which served also to enhance the power and glory of the pharaoh), or of placing it in a cave in a remote valley— robbers found their way into most of the tombs. But in many instances the measures taken were at least partly effective, so that archeologists often find the deceased and his earthly possessions almost as they were left thousands of years ago. In some of the cave tombs, for instance, where the cave kept out dampness and decay, animals and insects, the objects were so well preserved that even a fan made of ostrich plumes has been found in perfect condition.

We have long abandoned hope that objects so well preserved as those in Egyptian tombs will ever be found

4156

KING
TUTENKHAMO.

in the Land of the Two Rivers. The ancient inhabitants of that country, as we know from discoveries at Ur and Kish, also wanted to have with them for use in their future life the things they most loved. They too surrounded themselves with all their cherished belongings; they went even a step farther and had buried with themselves their chariots, a bodyguard of soldiers, and a good number, if not all, of their wives. Rather barbarous, one might say, but the burials to which I refer were very ancient; they antedated Tutenkhamon by about fifteen hundred years.

As in Egypt, the inhabitants of Mesopotamia had to contend with the danger of tomb-robbers. They had no stone in the land, so pyramids were out of the question. There were no mountains and, consequently, no caves. Nevertheless, they found a way that should have been more effective than it has proved to be. An immense hole was dug in the ground, and the tomb was placed within it as deep as possible. After the burial ceremonies had been completed, the ground was again leveled off, and very soon all traces of the exact spot disappeared completely. How the robbers found it out is a mystery to me, but they did find it. The royal tombs at Ur were completely rifled, and the richest of those discovered intact belonged to an obscure personage whose name was not even recorded in any of the historical documents we possess. After reaching the royal tombs, the robbers did not even think it worth while to continue their search. And yet from the treasures recovered in that one tomb we can form a vague idea of what we have missed.

The practice of hiding royal tombs deep in the ground

A WARRIOR'S SOLID GOLD HELMET FROM UR

is a great handicap for modern excavators. To dig into the soil of Mesopotamia to a depth of twenty to twenty-five meters is, of course, out of the question. There is no hope that documents may be found describing the exact locations of such tombs. We can only hope for a fortunate chance, but the probability is that the Mesopotamian kings will continue to sleep in peace for many centuries to come.

But there is more. If the ancient burial chambers were

not placed even deeper than they actually are, it was not because of lack of laborers or desire for economy. The deeper one goes, the greater the moisture, and I am certain that in many instances the idea of going deeper had to be abandoned because underground water would have filled up the newly made excavation. Even when the tomb was finally completed, if it was not actually under water, it was certainly surrounded by very moist ground. All perishable objects would disintegrate and be destroyed in the course of a few decades. What survive to our day are objects of gold, silver, copper, and stone. Of the royal chariots are found only the nails that fastened the leather strips around the wooden wheels and some bits of decoration, the bones of the animals, and the metal

BURIED WITH THEIR MASTER IN A "ROYAL TOMB" AT UR

bits in their mouths. The soldiers have their weapons, the court ladies their golden hair ornaments and jewels. All the rest has disappeared not only from these special tombs but doubtless also from all others that have remained undiscovered. We knew this long ago, and we are perfectly resigned to the fact that we will never unearth in Mesopotamia anything to compare with the Tutenkhamon finds. But, if this is so, why should we consider Mesopotamia such fertile ground for archeological investigations? There are many possible answers to this question: the great antiquity of the land, the many different civilizations that flourished there side by side, and so forth. But the answer can be given in a few words only: the so-called Babylonian clay tablets.

AN IMPERISHABLE DOCUMENT

Chapter 2

CLAY is practically indestructible. If it is of good quality and has been baked, everyone knows that it can withstand the elements without suffering in the least. Jars made of all sorts of clay, baked in different ways and with different degrees of heat, are found in the ruins of nearly all ancient cities—so much so that in many lands practically the only evidence for dating an ancient ruin is the sherds of pottery. The texture of the clay, the glaze, the shape of the object, the type of baking it has undergone, the decoration—all give a definite message to the people who can read them.

But, while it is well known that baked clay is indestructible, it is not common knowledge that tablets or jars, even when unbaked, will keep indefinitely. For this, of course, we need a good kind of clay, and Babylonian scribes praised the water-cleaned clay which they recognized as indispensable to their civilization. We also hear of clay being washed intentionally, and at times such a process must have been employed for the clay that was used for very fine pottery or for important tablets. The process was simple. The clay was placed in water and stirred. All bits of wood, straw, leaves, and the like floated on top and could easily be thrown away. Little pebbles, sand, or other impurities sank and immediately deposited themselves at the bottom of the vessel. After the water had been removed, the top part of the clay was perfectly clean and free from impurities of all kinds.

But even this process was generally unnecessary. The rivers themselves deposited almost yearly a good stratum of clay along their banks. Floating impurities had already been carried away by the receding waters, or deposited here and there in shallow pools. Stones and sand were necessarily at the bottom. I once watched some workmen wading in the freshly laid mud, scooping up with their hands the top clay, and piling it in little mounds to be taken away; it was evidently reserved for fine pottery, since tablets are no longer made. The coarser clay could be gathered later, thoroughly mixed with chopped straw, and used for making bricks.

A little brick of clay, if in pure condition and well kneaded, may lie buried in the moist ground for thousands of years and not only retain its shape but harden again, when dried, to the same consistency as before. If covered with writing, as is generally the case with Babylonian tablets, one can take the small unbaked tablet and brush it vigorously with a good stiff brush without the slightest fear of damaging its surface. All adhering impurities, with the exception of some mineral salts, are brushed away. If the salt incrustations should be too many and render decipherment impossible, then all one has to do is to bake the tablet thoroughly. After baking, it can be immersed in water, subjected to acids, or even boiled, and it will be as fine and clean as on the day it was first made and written upon.

There is one interesting peculiarity about clay; in drying it shrinks considerably. When perfectly dry clay

UNCOVERING AN ANCIENT LIBRARY

tablets are placed in a jar and buried in wet ground, they will gradually absorb moisture and swell. The tablets become too large for the jar, but the best they can do is to push into every available cranny until finally their shapes are completely distorted. An archeologist who comes upon a jar like that will be wise not to attempt to extricate the tablets before they have had a chance to dry out completely and shrink again. Even after this, the now distorted documents may be difficult to remove without damage. The discoverer may have to break the jar to get them out, but the damage is not great, since one can easily repair the jar again by means of a special kind of gluc, and in any case the archeological value of the contents is out of all proportion to that of the container. The thousands of tablets buried in the ruins of an old city may therefore be somewhat damaged as far as their shape is concerned, especially if buried together with hard objects. But, even if somewhat distorted, they are nearly always readable.

Worse is their fate if, while they are soft in the moist ground, they find themselves in the path of small rodents or earthworms. Many earthworms, who lived perhaps a millennium ago, have immortalized themselves through their work. In the course of their wanderings underground they encounter a tablet. Sometimes, in spite of the tablet's comparative softness, they find the clay too hard for their liking; and so they go around the obstacle, eating as they go, until they reach softer ground. At other times they pass right through, undaunted by the added difficulty they meet. We used to call these earthworms that damaged our tablets the original bookworms.

I greatly admired those who went straight through, leaving a clean hole in their wake. The damage they did was not great—perhaps one sign or two on either side of the tablet. Less determined ones, feeling their way all along the surface hoping to find a soft spot, left a long welt with the complete destruction of whole lines of writing. Even in the case of earthworms I prefer those which go right through to their goal without being diverted by difficulties.

Archeologists working in Iraq at the present time have different ideas regarding the best way to deal with tablets when they find them in a fresh and easily damageable condition. When I first started excavating, I tried different systems, but there is only one that I can recommend. As soon as found, the tablet must be cleaned of the surrounding dirt before being touched with the hand. When its condition is such that it can be handled, it should be picked up carefully, wrapped in thin paper, and wrapped again in heavier paper. Then the little bundle—on which all indications as to provenience, date, and the like, have been recorded promptly—should be taken into a house and left to dry slowly in the shade for at least fifteen days. Since it will shrink during this process, the packages will become quite loose and cannot be handled at all. After fifteen days the tablet can be rewrapped in the final package, since by that time it has already shrunk to its original size. At no time should the tablet be exposed to the sun, either while being extricated or when in its package. It will dry too quickly and go to pieces. If these simple precautions are observed, every document will be saved, ready perhaps to be baked at a a later time if this should be advisable.

Sometimes the Babylonians themselves baked their documents. Some of the more important business contracts have undergone this process so as to be absolutely safe from destruction. The same applies also to tablets in the libraries that were supposed to be used and read frequently. But unfortunately a great number of the documents are still unbaked, and excavations in Iraq will always have to be carried on with great care.

The results, however, will be sure to repay any extra amount of watchfulness. For think of it: almost every scrap of writing, even if it was unimportant or discarded, is waiting for us somewhere in the ruins of those ancient cities. Suppose you throw a letter in the wastebasket today. Where will it be tomorrow? But the letter which a man threw into the wastebasket four thousand years ago, and which was the next day dumped onto the refuse heap, is still there and may some day come to light!

These little clay tablets, with all sorts of records, began to pile up in great numbers early in the third millennium B.C. and continued to accumulate until the beginning of the Christian Era. We have thus an unbroken line of documents covering all phases of knowledge throughout those centuries. Through them, we can follow changes in religious beliefs, economic conditions, and customs in daily life. In fact, through them we can and we will resurrect the old civilizations in the minutest details. The work has begun with astonishing results. In these pages I shall try to give an idea of what we have already recovered and leave to the imagination what else we may confidently expect.

Chapter 3

THE modern name for the land that approximately covers ancient Babylonia and Assyria is Iraq. This name was resurrected a few years ago, for it is not by any means new. It may be translated "littoral" or "coastland," and, if one has in mind the banks of the rivers which wash the land, it is, as we shall see, singularly apt.

Iraq is bounded on the east by a chain of mountains that separates it from Iran, or Persia; on the north, by a series of ranges cutting it off from Armenia and Asia Minor; on the west and south, by steppes and deserts. It is therefore well isolated from surrounding lands. But it is a fertile spot, easily adapted to agricultural pursuits and practically made to order to be the cradle of a great civilization.

Its isolation holds true to a certain extent even today. But what must it have been like in ancient times when the caravans, attempting to reach the lands of Syria and Palestine, had before them a journey of some five hundred miles across a waterless desert? The road was bad and dangerous, and sometimes they had to take a somewhat longer route and skirt the mountains to the north in order to get water. Of course, conditions today are different. With the advantage of the automobile one can make a trip across the desert from Damascus to Baghdad in

"THE LAZILY MOVING, CHOCOLATE-COLORED EUPHRATES"

something like fifteen hours. Traveling by airplane, one may leave Cairo early in the morning, breakfast in Palestine, and dine in Baghdad!

Why, one may ask, is the name Iraq appropriate? It is a truism that there would be no Egypt except for its river, the Nile, whose periodical inundations give fertility to the adjacent fields. The same is even more true of Iraq. While the land of Egypt, with the exception of part of the Delta, would be there even without the Nile —though it would be as dry as the Sahara Desert—much of Iraq would not even exist but for its two famous rivers, the Tigris and the Euphrates. A large part of the land is made up of silt carried down by these rivers from the mountains to the north. This work of depositing and therefore increasing the extent of the land has gone on since time immemorial and is continuing even today. The two rivers in ancient times reached the Persian Gulf independently. So much more silt has been carried down since the time when they joined their forces that the gulf today is ninety miles away from the junction. Ancient cities that used to be close to the sea are now far inland, and the new ground, all formed after the collapse of the ancient civilizations, is absolutely devoid of any traces of them. Not a sherd of ancient pottery or a fragment of a tablet can ever be expected from the newly made land.

Since much of the country has been made by the deposits of the rivers, it is necessarily quite flat. The streams could never pile up dirt in the shape of a hill; water will always follow one level, and the entire plain will be of uniform height. Since the rivers never encountered mountains or sharp embankments, at the period of inundation they often changed their beds and ran more to the right or left of their old courses. This helped in further

NEBUCHADNEZZAR'S QUAY STILL FRONTS THE TIGRIS AT BAGHDAD

leveling the land. The silt carried by the rivers was splendid ground for cultivation; hence from earliest antiquity settlements were made all around the rivers, especially where a regular inundation could be expected to fertilize the fields just as the Nile periodically fertilizes Egypt.

But the ancient Babylonians soon found that they did not need to wait for inundations and base their future on the whims of the rivers. They could easily regulate the flow of water to suit their particular needs. Great canals were built connecting the rivers themselves and their equally important tributaries. From one large canal other canals branched off, carrying surplus water wherever it was needed; still smaller irrigation ditches swung off from the secondary canals until the whole land was a

MODERN ARABS DIG THEIR IRRIGATION CANAL

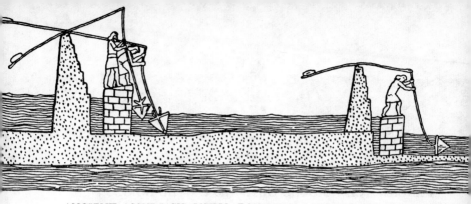

ANCIENT ASSYRIANS USING EGYPTIAN METHOD OF IRRIGATION

web of watercourses. These not only distributed the water where it was most needed but also minimized the danger of destructive inundations. The Tigris and the Euphrates, which had done the work of building up the land, were also made to continue the task and bring it to the highest degree of productivity.

Digging the very large canals was extremely expensive, required a great number of men, and was generally undertaken by the government, that is, by the kings. These monarchs praised themselves for their good work, and the canals were perennial monuments to the wisdom and paternal care of the men who boasted of having built them. As a matter of fact, they were actually built by the poor citizens, who were obliged either to contribute their own personal labor or to pay for them with their taxes. It is exactly the same as the building of a great modern highway or an immense dam—one man gets the credit, but the taxpayers foot the bill. Just as in the case of our modern highways, the canals had to be taken care of all the time; otherwise silt would have filled them up. Gangs of workmen were therefore constantly employed

27

AN ANCIENT CITY MOUND OUTLINED ON THE HORIZON

in maintaining the level of the canals. Governors of the provinces or high officials were personally responsible for keeping them in good order. Secondary branches were also under the direct attention of the provincial authorities, while the smallest ditches were tended by the owner of the land through which they passed. If any break caused a needless waste of water or damage to the surrounding fields, the owner was personally answerable and had to make restitution for all loss caused by his negligence. Naturally the great cities were placed either close to the two big rivers and their affluents or very near the large canals which were navigable by the small boats carrying goods throughout the land. Thus the canals served the triple purpose of distributing the water, providing a means of flood control, and acting as highways of commerce.

If one travels over the land of Iraq by airplane, one can still see very clearly marked on the ground the ancient network of canals. One can also see grouped alongside them the ruins of the old cities. Many times I have been asked the questions: How do archeologists find the ancient cities? How do they know that the place where they dig is exactly the spot where an old city lay? The question should rather be: How can one who is not absolutely blind have any trouble whatsoever in choosing the right spot? Cities are all around. Every mound of dirt is a city. I have yet to find a place in the land of Iraq, except in the newly formed delta, on which one can stand and not see two or three cities clearly outlined on the horizon. The worry of the archeologist is not how to find a city but which one to choose out of the many that surround him on all sides.

For even in the field of archeology there is specialization, and each excavator has a definite purpose in mind. He does not dig at random just out of curiosity to see what will come out. In a land where civilization endured for many thousands of years he has to specialize to a certain extent. A man who is perfectly at home among the monuments of the late Greek period would find himself at a total loss on a prehistoric mound. Consequently, each excavator will try to look very carefully before deciding.

For an expert who can read the signs there is little

THE MOUND OF MEGIDDO ("ARMAGEDDON"), SCENE OF MANY BATTLES, VIEWS A PEACEFUL PROCESSION OF NATIVES

UNCOVERING SHERDS AND POTS—CLUES TO THE ANCIENT INHABITANTS

chance of failure. Fashions changed in ancient times, though not so rapidly as they do today. Within the same group of people pottery came to be developed to such an extent that perhaps the later was better and more decorative than the earlier; or perhaps the opposite was true. With the introduction of metals the artists of the time discarded clay vessels as the mediums for their inspiration. They concentrated on copper or bronze and completely neglected pottery. That was relegated to the kitchen and the more humble uses. Thus we find that in some places the pottery of the old period was very good and that of a later period was rough and of poor workmanship. We have different styles of pottery within the same cultural group. But we have also a wandering of the people. New immigrants enter and introduce new fashions. As a result of all this, the man who can correctly interpret a few sherds of broken vases has a sure clue to the period and to the kind of population that inhabited the place. Then, again, metals came to be used at different periods: bronze later than copper, and iron later than bronze. And so fragments of metal are of assistance in the dating. Writing changed as much as anything else, and a little piece of an inscription, even though it contains nothing of a historical character, can be dated from the shape of the signs. Thus we see that if a man knows his job he has sufficient help to find exactly what he wants.

RESTORING JARS FROM INNUMERABLE FRAGMENTS

But, of course, walking on top of a mound, one sees only the vestiges of the latest civilization on that mound. If the top dates from the Persian period, that does not mean that everything contained in that little hill will date from the same period. The deeper one goes, the more ancient the city which will be uncovered.

At this point it is necessary to answer a question which is very frequently asked of archeologists: How is it that sometimes several cities are found on the same spot? How could different cities be superimposed so that we have a Greek city on top, a Babylonian city in the middle, and a Sumerian city on the bottom? The perplexity which gives rise to such questions is easily understood and has been chiefly caused by archeologists who have been too quick to announce the discovery of a "Mound of Seven Cities." However, it is the simplest thing in the world to comprehend how such a mound came to be.

If one goes to Rome and looks at the ancient Forum, one immediately notices that the old level is lower by several meters than that of the modern street. Still, as it is the same old Rome, could we not speak of the modern city as being superimposed on the old one? The level of a city grows with time, and the same phenomenon that one sees in Rome may be seen in any other ancient city.

In the Orient such a condition can be observed better than anywhere else. The people had to contend with a flat land which might at any time be inundated by the rivers. A very common precaution, therefore, was to build a little mound of clay that would raise the foundations of the houses a trifle above the level of the ground. We thus have the beginning of the mound. The houses were built with walls of unbaked bricks and plastered with clay. The roofs of the private dwellings were generally thatched and covered with a thick layer of clay that prevented the rain from filtering through. Each year, at the conclusion of the rainy season, the plaster on the outside walls had to be renewed. The roofs also got a fresh coating of clay. But all the clay that had been washed down from walls and roof was deposited in the street; naturally, the street level gradually increased in height. Further, in ancient cities there was no provision for the disposal of refuse; if one ate shellfish, the shells were thrown into the street to remain there. If a change was made in the plan of the house and a wall demolished, all the bricks from that wall would go into the street. I remember that once, when walking through Baghdad, I had to go up and down over little mounds of bricks and mortar that had been thrown into the street from houses, to remain there forever. Add to all this the fact that adobe buildings are rather short-lived. After a certain time the walls begin to cave in, and the expense of keeping them repaired is more than that of tearing them down and rebuilding on the same site—but the new house built on the ruins of the preceding one is necessarily a little higher. Thus, through a series of natural developments, the street level gradually rises.

Sometimes unforeseen events greatly assist this slow process of growth. A great conflagration may level out a complete section of the city overnight. An enemy may destroy the whole place and abandon it, or rebuild it perhaps the next year or many years after. A city may thus remain uninhabited for some time, only to be settled

A STEP-TRENCH REVEALING ANCIENT CULTURAL LAYERS

Here, layer by layer, over five thousand years of history are graphically represented. Each "period" is marked by the products of a single group of traditions in the manufacture of pottery, metal, stone, bone, and other tools. The periods may each contain several levels of occupation. The sketches show objects which are typical for their period, and occur only sporadically, if at all, in any other period. Thus by a careful check of the objects from a given floor, the archeologist can

PERIOD

I.   A.D. 600–300. The level of an early Christian church. On a near-by site are even later Byzantine ruins and bronze crosses of the priests.

II.   A.D. 300–64 B.C. A village partly contemporary with Paul and early Christian missionary activity in Antioch. Coins of the Caesars and Roman lamps.

III.   ca. 64–500 B.C. An occupation of the period of the Persian Empire and of the Greek empires which followed the conquests of Alexander the Great.

IV.   ca. 500–1000 B.C. Layers of the Syrian Hittite kingdom, contemporary with the later Assyrian Empire and the Babylonian Nebuchadnezzar. Hittite hieroglyphs.

V.   ca. 1000–1200 B.C. Ceramic traces of the "Peoples of the Sea," some of whom are known as the Philistines, others as the Achaeans who sacked Troy.

VI.   ca. 1200–1600 B.C. A period rich in imported pottery of Cypriote and Aegean type, contemporary with the culture at Ugarit.

VII.   ca. 1600–1900 B.C. The beginning of marked technological advances in the second millennium B.C. Grotesque "mother-goddess" figurines are characteristic of this period.

VIII.   ca. 1900–2000 B.C. A period of transition (probably of a relatively short time) during which certain distinct types of pottery were manufactured.

IX.   ca. 2000–2300 B.C. A time of brilliant work in metal and pottery, climaxing the technological achievements of the third millennium B.C.

X.   ca. 2300–2600 B.C. The beginnings of a range of goblets and small drinking vessels; a period rich in connections with the south and east.

XI.   ca. 2600–3000 B.C. A range marked by a fine red-and-black pottery series, by excellent metalwork, and by cylinder seals of Mesopotamian type.

XII.   ca. 3000–3500 B.C. A period of technological advancement, at the end of which appear the earliest known castings of human figures in metal. Links to both Egypt and Mesopotamia.

XIII.   ca. 3500–3900 B.C. Levels yielding rather drab pottery but the earliest types of tectonically conceived metal tools. The technological traditions have links to the east.

GAP

XIV.   ca. 5000–5500 B.C.?? Traces of materials in the range of the earliest known villages of Syro-Cilicia. Hand-made, polished pottery; simple tools in bone and flint.

VIRGIN SOIL   *Six Feet under the Present Water Level.*

establish their sequence, just as one might differentiate between the "buggy wheel" and the "automobile tire" periods in American history by digging through a city dump. The step-trench shown above was one of the means by which an Oriental Institute expedition established, for the first time, a complete relative chronology for North Syria. Comparable results could be obtained at almost any Near Eastern mound, either by similar step-trenches or by vertical soundings.

A "MOUND OF SEVEN CITIES," MODERN ARBIL

again either by a different race or by the same one. At any rate, under the new occupancy the level continues to rise, and this constant increase in height never ends. Sometimes the old city, which is perched on top of the artificial hill, proves to be too small for an increased population. Then there is an overflow, and a new settlement is built on the plain at the base of the mound; this outer city likewise begins to grow slowly and reach higher. Even on the very top of one of these artificial mounds the level is not always the same. In one place, where there was a large courtyard, well paved and drained, there would be a very small percentage of growth. On the opposite side of the "tell," as such a city mound is called, there may have been built a royal palace, with very high and thick walls; the ruins of that one building would already make a little mound on top of the big one.

There are in Iraq today a number of cities still occupied which are built over the ruins of many previous occupations. Two of these are Arbil and Kirkuk. In the case of the former especially, one has to ascend a long ramp before one can reach the top of the city. From there one commands a splendid view of the surrounding plains. High walls prevent the loose ground from falling down the side and endangering the lower city, and the mound of Arbil is destined to remain safe from the elements for a good many hundred years. In Kirkuk the old mound still preserves its original shape, and in many places the rains have so washed out the sides of the tell as to imperil the houses on top.

Where such a thing as this has happened, the archeologist can obtain an excellent view of the stratification of the old mound. If he can interpret it, the story is just as plain as the one that our geologists can read so easily when they observe the earth's strata. Here one can see the baked bricks that once formed a pavement, sticking out of the clay and marking out a straight line which clearly indicates one of the levels. Jars, either broken or intact, may also be visible either in their original position or thrown around at random. Then comes a little stratum of mixed debris, consisting of broken bricks, sherds of pottery, sea shells, and refuse. Again another series of bricks in perfect alignment: a later pavement

MODERN KIRKUK RESTS ON THE DEBRIS OF MILLENNIUMS

under which the debris had been thrown in order to form a good foundation. Over this pavement perhaps a lot of ashes and charcoal: mute evidence of a fire that destroyed the houses. Perhaps, then, some clean clay tossed about by the winds, indicating a pause—no doubt when the city had been abandoned for a period of years. Higher again the foundations of a new wall, followed perhaps by a third pavement.

If the city was an important one and the dwelling-place of a king, the pavements will be made with bricks stamped with the name of the king. In that case there is no trouble for the archeologist; he knows perfectly well that "Pavement A" will date, let us say, 2000 B.C., and the one immediately over it, which we may call "B," 1767 B.C. All the objects found on the lower pavement probably belong to the intervening period.

Thus it is that in the same city an original population that we cannot perhaps identify very well may be dispossessed by the Sumerians, who remained there for a certain length of time and then in their turn were ousted or absorbed by some other peoples. And so we may have first the unknown settlement, then a Sumerian city, then a Babylonian city, and thereafter continue through the Persian, Greek, Parthian, Sasanian, and Moslem strata. We may even find a medieval town above these, and then on the very top the existing modern city: "The Hill of the Seven Cities." But the city is always the same; it is only the people who change.

Many of the old towns had already been abandoned in very remote periods. Tablets dating 1500 B.C. speak of ancient ruins which are mentioned simply to locate properly fields or districts. If we can go back another thousand years to the inhabitants of 2500 B.C., we shall still see ancient and abandoned cities surrounding them. How far back this process might go it is impossible to say.

A modern archeologist, as we mentioned above, has a pretty clear idea of what he wants. If he is interested in the oldest civilizations, he would make a very big mistake if he dug up a city that started in the early period but continued into Greek times; he would have to dig for years and years in a field of activity which would interest him very little and for the study of which he would perhaps not be qualified. If he wants a very early city, he will have to find one that was abandoned in early antiquity. Then he can start his work and immediately get at the period he desires. Conversely, it would be foolish for a man who wants the Greek period to start digging on a tell that was never inhabited in Greek times. The more he dug, the farther away he would get from the period of his interest.

For these reasons careful archeologists examine the mounds as thoroughly as possible before even putting a spade into the ground. If they can "read" the pottery, if they know about writing and have a general knowledge of the civilizations of the different historical periods, they are not likely to make mistakes. But unless this preparatory work is well done, a ludicrous result may follow.

Chapter 4

A TOURIST who goes through Iraq today, unless he happens upon some locality where excavations are actually being conducted, would be likely to visit a large part of the land without even suspecting that most of the little mounds which surround him are ancient cities. No great monuments would ever attract his attention, and he could never imagine that at one spot in his aimless wanderings he might be treading on what was formerly the market place of a metropolis or even the ruins of a once-famous temple. The land is practically deserted now, and he could never suspect that the desert around him was at one time a blooming garden or that the silence now enveloping him was long ago broken by the many sounds of an active civilization and by the voices of many different tongues.

If the tourist of today, after all that has been written about the ancient civilizations of Babylonia and Assyria, fails to get an accurate conception of what the past was, one can easily imagine that the first travelers crossed and recrossed the land without suspecting that they were close to the historical sites of Babylon and Nineveh. Even scientifically minded travelers who knew from the Bible of the existence of these two cities, and attempted to find them, several times passed over their very ruins without knowing it. Inscribed clay tablets were found by natives in the course of their daily labor and were offered to travelers, but these inscriptions were neglected, since no one could ever imagine that so many little combinations of nail-like impressions could represent any system of writing. It is to the everlasting credit of the acute and intelligent Pietro della Valle that, as one of the first to recognize writing on the little "bricks," he acquired one of them and sent it to the Kircherian Museum. There it is now, the first cuneiform document ever placed in a European museum. But not all could be expected to be as keen-minded as this famous traveler, and for many years learned men debated whether these little impressions had to be considered as simple decorations or as an unknown and mysterious system of writing.

In my opinion the European scholars during those years remained away behind the "ignorant" Mohammedans. The Koran speaks of the existence of "bricks baked in Hell and written by the demons," and there is no doubt in my mind that the reference applies to the many inscribed bricks that are found throughout Meso-

"NINEVEH SHALL BECOME A WASTE"

THE VILLAGE OF KHORSABAD SEEN FROM SARGON'S PALACE MOUND

potamia. The explanation that Mohammed gave for the provenience of these bricks may not have been quite correct, but at least he knew that they had to do with writing!

Gradually with the passing of years it came to be known that Mesopotamia was the ancient land of Babylonia and Assyria, but even this did not cause any great rush of excavators. The Assyrians, it was said, were a notoriously wicked people, and the Lord had decided to destroy them and wipe out the memory of them from the face of the earth; to resurrect them would be nothing short of blasphemy! Who knows how long this attitude would have lasted had not an enterprising layman, Emile Botta, the French consul in Mosul, decided to inquire about the exact significance of some curious pieces of sculpture which had been discovered by natives on a big hill just opposite the city of Mosul. He began excavations, and the place proved to be the site of the ancient city Nineveh. His labors were rewarded by no important finds, but through his energy he succeeded in persuading the French government to help in the excavations. When the native Arabs found that Botta was interested in stone reliefs, they told him that a few miles away there was another hill in which such objects were to be discovered. Botta rushed there and found the reports to be correct; he began with great zeal to dig into the palace of King Sargon, in Khorsabad.

The first excavations were not conducted according to scientific canons. The excavator himself was seldom a scientist, and anyhow scientific methods—from the viewpoint of modern archeology—had yet to be evolved. It is unreasonable to accuse Botta, for instance, of not having conducted his excavations according to approved standards, since he was a pioneer in the field. Scientific canons for Mesopotamian archeology were developed after his time; but, whether we approve of everything he did or not, he worked with great energy and intense enthusiasm and succeeded in waking up the world to the fact that a great civilization was coming to light. Then the rush began. The English took up the abandoned work in Nineveh, while the French continued their activity in Khorsabad. Free-lance scientific explorers went all over the land trying to find out as much as they could. They were looking chiefly for large stone reliefs and colossal statues; if in the course of their excavations they found bricks and tablets, they were likely to disregard them completely and throw them away with the dirt.

SARGON'S CITY AT KHORSABAD AS EXCAVATED BY THE ORIENTAL INSTITUTE

But even the great stone reliefs were covered with strange groups of wedges; and this time there was no doubt but that they were inscriptions, though their contents were as much a mystery as before.

The key to the decipherment of the Egyptian hieroglyphics was given by the Rosetta Stone, which was found by the soldiers of Napoleon at the time of his attempted conquest of Egypt. The Rosetta Stone obviously contained the very same inscription, both in Greek and in the strange hieroglyphics which were known to have been used by the Egyptians. Starting from the known, slowly the hieroglyphs were made to yield their valuable secrets.

In the case of the cuneiform languages, something of the same kind happened. Travelers had noticed a number of inscriptions sculptured on rocks in Persia. Each inscription was repeated three times, in what we now know to be three separate languages: Old Persian, Babylonian, and Elamite. In each case the writing was of the character which we call cuneiform, that is, made by means of a combination of wedges. A close study of these different versions showed that the wedges were combined in different systems in the three versions. In one, the combination was simpler; it appeared much less confused, and the very same groups recurred much more often than in the other versions. Scholars decided that this version in which there was the smallest number of

UNCOVERING A GATEWAY AT KHORSABAD

groups must be written with an alphabet; each group of wedges must stand for a letter. The other writings were more complicated; the signs were so many and so varied that the versions containing them were set apart as being too difficult. Scholars' attention was, therefore, focused on the simplest of the three versions, and they tried to wrest the meanings hidden behind the curious nail- or wedge-like impressions.

It is impossible in this chapter to give anything but a brief summary of the steps which were taken by the ingenious pioneer decipherers. It had been called to the attention of a German high-school teacher that the writings of later Persian kings always began with the phrase, "So-and-so, the great king, the king of kings, son of So-and-

HIGH ON A PERSIAN MOUNTAINSIDE ARE THE SCULPTURES OF DARIUS THE GREAT

so. . . . ." He observed that in the simpler version of one of the inscriptions, groups of signs occurred more or less in the expected order. He began to fit a name of a king with what he thought should have been the Persian reading of the signs, and succeeded in reading "Darius, the great king, king of kings, son of Hystaspes." He thus settled the meanings of some signs, and other scholars helped him. The work was necessarily slow because in those times communication was more difficult than today, and many months were wasted by individual scholars on problems which had already been solved by their colleagues working independently. But eventually the scholars were able to announce that one of the versions had been read and that it was written in Old Persian. With that translation as a key they attacked the other two.

The decipherment of the Babylonian version presented many more difficulties because the writing was not at all alphabetic. Controversies raged among those pioneers, each trying to prove to the other that his theories alone were tenable. But slowly some agreement was obtained among the chief exponents of the new science until they could announce that the secret of the old Babylonian inscriptions had been solved.

But the world outside was still skeptical. How could other people know that the explanations now being offered were right? The scholars had to prove that they had actually found the key. A test was staged; four of them were given the very same inscription to translate, and the results of their work would show whether the new science had reached a sufficient stage of maturity to deserve some sort of public acceptance. These first Assyriologists

47

studied their texts and presented their conclusions. While the four translations differed in some details, still it was evident from the many points of agreement that Assyriology, as this new field of learning came to be called, had the right to be admitted into the circle of sciences.

Gradually progress was made, until now the Assyrian and Babylonian dialects present relatively few difficulties.

A WEIGHT STONE INSCRIBED IN THREE LANGUAGES—OLD PERSIAN, ELAMITE, AND BABYLONIAN

To be sure, there are persons who are still unconvinced, and from time to time some wild theorist publishes a book trying to prove that all decipherment is on the wrong track and that he alone has the real key. I received such a book just off the press a short time ago, and I thoroughly enjoyed glancing through it. Had the book appeared eighty years ago, it would have been excusable. Now it is fit only for the wastebasket.

While at present we cannot claim an absolute knowledge of the language because there are still a good many objects—such as plants, stones, drugs, instruments, and others—which will cause trouble for years to come, yet it is in its essentials as easy as most other languages or perhaps even easier. No longer does it need the help of its cognates to be understood. Indeed, the process is now reversed. Through it we understand better some of the other Semitic languages which closely resemble it, for it is the Assyrian word which can now be used to fix the exact meaning of the Hebrew word. Another strange thing has happened. Assyrian was formerly the "cognate" of Hebrew and was interesting principally because of its connections with the Bible. It was studied chiefly in order to find in the old inscriptions confirmation of the sacred texts, and for many years remained in the position of a poor relation. It had to be helped along with the crumbs that fell from the table of the older, more important language. Now the trend is quite the reverse; Assyrian literature is important in itself and would be of value even if we had no Hebrew Bible. At the same time, in schools and theological seminaries, the tendency is away from the study of Hebrew. And so it is that in some institutions Assyriology is already the center of attention!

Chapter 5

W E KNOW very little about the origin of the Sumerians. As yet we cannot even decide whether they were indigenous to the country of Mesopotamia or whether they came in from the outside, though the second hypothesis is the more probable and was considered a certainty for a good many years. Since we are not able to decide this question definitely, we find it also impossible to say whether the earliest attempts at writing were made in the land of Mesopotamia or outside. In fact, some people are beginning to doubt whether we are right in crediting the Sumerians with the invention of writing. However that may be, they certainly developed it along the special ways which later resulted in cuneiform writing; whether or not they started it we cannot yet say.

The Sumerians had a high regard for the art of writing and placed its invention at the very beginning of their civilization. Moreover, they considered that civilization as of great antiquity, and early texts speak with contempt of the nomads, who are described as "people who do not know houses and who do not cultivate wheat." But it is impossible to determine when and where the first attempt at writing was made. In this we are handicapped also by the consideration that at the very beginning clay may not have been used as a writing medium.

Looking at the subject as impartially as possible, we think the Sumerians developed their own system of writing. They did it by going through a very long and elaborate process. For there never was a first man who could sit down and say, "Now I am going to write." That supreme achievement of mankind, the one which makes possible the very existence of civilization by transferring to later generations the acquisitions of the earlier ones, was the result of a slow and natural development.

If one of the primitive artists sat down and made a picture of a gazelle, it was not writing. It was simply a work of art. If he had discovered the presence of gazelles in a certain place and drew the picture of one of them on a stone so as to tell his friends that it was good hunting ground, then his picture was no longer a work of art; it was a message. That one picture simply says, "Here are gazelles." The message might contain more than one picture. He might put a lion together with the gazelle, and the message would be interpreted as meaning "Good hunting ground, but watch out!" Such being the case, we cannot even begin to determine whether an early picture is actual writing or merely the product of an artistic mind. However, people soon began to realize that messages could be conveyed by means of pictures. Hence we have to see in picture-writing the first step in the development of all writing.

If, at a later date, an alphabet appears to come out of nowhere, that also must be the result of a previous evolution which extended perhaps through millenniums. No man could ever have written a single letter of the alphabet unless he had been already familiar with some sort of

AN ANCIENT SUMERIAN

A MODERN ARAB

well-developed system of writing. And so the early Sumerians, or someone before them, far back in antiquity, began to write by means of little pictures.

It was easy to represent concrete ideas. If one wished to indicate a man, one simply drew the picture of a man, and the same would apply to a star, a foot, a tree, or what not. An abstract idea was more difficult to represent, but the association of ideas came to one's aid. A foot does not always indicate a certain part of the human anatomy; it sometimes gives the idea of walking. The picture of a star does signify a star, but it can also be used to mean the sky where stars are placed or the gods who are in heaven and are more or less identified with the heavenly bodies. By combining pictures, one could get also some other ideas. The picture of a mouth plus the picture of a piece of bread in it means "to eat"; the same mouth with a representation of water inside it necessarily means "to drink."

It is possible, therefore, to give quite long and complicated messages simply through the use of pictures, and in some cases this pictographic writing is so convenient that it has not been abandoned even in the present day. If a bottle of medicine shows a picture of skull and crossbones, one who looks at it will immediately get a complete message, "If you drink this, you will die!" That also can be read by anyone, whether he has gone to school or not; it is not confined to any one language and can be easily understood by a variety of people speaking entirely different languages. This same advantage has caused some other symbols to travel through the world and be accepted everywhere as pure ideographs. These are the common figures for numerals; when one sees the figure "5," one immediately has an idea of a certain number of units, and that number is the same whether the reader is a Frenchman, an Englishman, or an Italian.

Through a skilful combination of true pictures and symbols which represent ideas, it is possible to write down sentences which can be understood. A good many of our most fascinating puzzles today are nothing but ideographic writing. However, writing by means of pictures and symbols will always be open to the very great objection that three readers may interpret the same writing and get three entirely different messages. There is too much left to the imagination to assure the exactness that all writing should have. Moreover, in many cases it is absolutely impossible to represent through symbols an abstract idea such as "honesty." Again, suppose an ancient scholar, who knew only how to write through pictures, were asked to write down the personal name of some individual, like Kuraka, which could not be put down in symbols. The first thing he could have thought of doing would have been to make a picture of the individual in question so closely resembling the original that no one would ever mistake it. But this would have been impossible, and also would have required of the reader a personal acquaintance with the personage mentioned. Obviously this system would fail.

But necessity is the mother of invention. All the Sumerian pictures were inevitably associated with the words by which they were read. A mountain was pronounced *kur*, and so the sign for mountain necessarily suggested the sound *kur*. The sign for water was read *a*,

IS THIS WRITING?

Actually the gazelles were drawn by a scribe during a "breathing-spell" from his prescribed task—cutting an inscription, the wedges of which may be seen on the right.

and the sign for mouth was pronounced *ka*. These different sounds came to be closely associated with the pictures of the things that they indicated. The only way to write a thing which could not be otherwise represented was to group together two or three signs, the combined sound of which would indicate either the personal name or the special idea to be expressed. And so, if the scribe wanted to write the name "Kuraka," all he had to do was to write the sign for mountain, then the sign for water and the sign for mouth, and promptly forget the original ideas of mountain, water, and mouth. To help the reader, the scribe would put in front a little mark that indicated, "Watch out, what follows is a personal name; do not read it 'mountain' or 'water' or whatever it is!" In other cases a warning sign simply said that what followed was the name of a river or the name of a mountain or of a plant or a stone or what not. These warning signs are what we call "determinatives" because they help us to determine the character of what follows.

Going back to the writing, this special departure in using the sound indicated by the picture rather than the idea indicated by that picture was a tremendous step forward. I am certain that in the beginning it was taken because it could not be helped; and it was limited to the most necessary cases. But the scholars of antiquity must have realized that, if they could represent sounds instead of ideas, they could transmit their message with the precision so highly desired. It was no longer compulsory to give just the idea of the verb "to go." One could write down "I went" or "I shall go." Gradually this highly important innovation began to gain strength. It did not immediately dethrone the old ideograph; the latter had so many good points and could give such an accurate idea with only one picture that it was kept out of convenience up to the very end of the development of cuneiform characters. But in the case of verbs especially the new phonetic writing displaced the old method.

We shall continue later with the adventures of the little pictures in respect to the ideas or sounds they convey, but we must now take up another series of adventures connected with their shape. In the beginning, of course, each writer made his pictures as complete and as beautiful as he wished. Still it was in many cases a great waste of time to put in a lot of unnecessary detail. Enterprising souls began to speculate on the question of how to represent an object, let us say a falcon or a star, with a minimum number of strokes. What part of the picture had to be stereotyped, so to speak, in order to prevent anyone from confusing a falcon with a goose? Thus, gradually in the main, the different pictures lost a good part of their beauty, retaining just enough of the essential features to be clearly identified.

There are few texts in Assyria or in Babylonia which give us very early writing. A few hundred clay documents, and one or two stone tablets, are the earliest we possess, but even on these many of the signs are later developments of earlier forms. And it is quite possible, as we said before, that clay was not used for the most ancient writings. In the ruins of some ancient cities in central Asia a large number of long strips of wood covered with writing have been found. Did the old Sumerians employ something analogous? If so, no wonder the early writings have completely disappeared! The Sumerian might have used some other kind of perishable material—the result would have been the same. We should still be entirely in the dark concerning the earliest steps in the art of writing.

EXAMPLES OF EXTREMELY EARLY PICTURE-WRITING

A second adventure was met by the poor pictures They were all thrown on their backs! Originally the writing began at the upper right-hand corner and moved down, as in Chinese, with the objects portrayed all facing to the right. Then for some uncertain reason—probably a practical one, such as the way in which the object being written upon was held in the hand—the characters were turned ninety degrees counterclockwise. Hence a tremendous revolution occurred. All the men standing found themselves on their backs, the trees were all thrown down,

59

the birds and animals pretty nearly lost their shapes. This was an adventure that would have completely upset the artistic sense of the early writers, but by this time a picture was· merely a symbol, and artistic beauty was completely neglected.

Something worse was still to come. When the original writing material, whatever it may have been, was abandoned and clay substituted, it was soon found that one could make a picture in the clay much more quickly and better by impressing than by scratching. Therefore a stylus, which was perhaps only a straight piece of reed with a triangular end, was used to impress the pictures in the fresh clay. An unexpected result came about: all curved lines had to go! The stylus would best produce only short straight lines! And so a circle had to be broken into a series of straight lines and therefore was no longer a circle; a fine sweeping curve had to become a series of short strokes one after the other, and so on.

The early scribes did their best to make their pictures resemble the original objects as closely as possible by combining all sorts of wedges. But it was a Herculean task, and the results were not very gratifying. The pictures were disappearing more and more in spite of all efforts to keep them alive. Gradually with the passing of centuries the attempt to preserve them was given up. Why try to represent a plow by means of twelve little wedges when six would do? Why put in all those extra flourishes when we can recognize the sign now? The picture as such was entirely given up. All that the scribes tried to keep apart were the signs which had developed from the previous pictures. There was no longer the idea of preventing the *picture* of a goose from being confused with that of a hawk. The chief concern now was to keep the many *signs* from becoming confused with one another.

The last and most terrible adventure of the pictures also came with the practice of efficiency. Why turn the hand in all possible directions, first to the left, then upright, then to the extreme right? It was tiresome and took a lot of time. And so the wedges used in making the pictures were divided into a few classes: perpendicular (𒁹), horizontal (▷—), and oblique (⟨ or ╱). No sign would ever go perpendicularly from the bottom upward, horizontally from right to left, or in a slanting position downward from right to left. Such movements were taboo as being too difficult for the scribe. To these three types of wedges another one was added which looked something like an arrowhead and could be made with the tip of the stylus (⟨). These four types of wedges had to serve for all the pictures; no others were allowed.

This was the very end. Not one of the signs of the later period, after all these adventures, resembles in the least the picture from which it originated. A good many of them not only lost all resemblance to their prototypes but they acquired phonetic values which are not even reminiscent of the original ones. Apart from some rare holdover such as a sign denoting a very common thing— and which could therefore be written down more quickly than the long phonetic name of this same thing—ideographic writing disappeared from everyday usage. No one, after looking at a late Babylonian tablet, would ever deny it. Through what a long evolution the signs had passed!

Original pictograph	Pictograph in position of later cuneiform	Early Babylonian	Assyrian	Original or derived meaning
				bird
				fish
				donkey
				ox
				sun day
				grain
				orchard
				to plow to till
				boomerang to throw to throw down
				to stand to go

THE ORIGIN AND DEVELOPMENT OF A FEW CUNEIFORM
CHARACTERS

Thus out of the many changes to which the physical shapes of the signs were subjected there grew almost a modern type of writing—unlike Egyptian hieroglyphic, which remained a picture writing nearly to the end of Egyptian civilization. And let us remember that the determining element behind all this development was clay, the writing medium.

Before we entered into the series of changes which made a picture unrecognizable, we were discussing the old ideographic signs when they were on the verge of standing for certain sounds and of ridding themselves of the restriction of representing one idea only. We had already said that, in order to express abstract ideas, concrete signs were used. The sign for foot meant "foot," but it meant also "to go," "to stand," etc. However, while the sign was always the same, the picture of a foot when it was to be read "to go" was read with the special sound which meant "to go," and when it was intended to indicate the idea of "standing," it was read in an entirely different way. We thus find that every one of the pictures came to be associated with three or four ideas, and therefore with three or four sounds.

The ancient Sumerian language was chiefly monosyllabic, and so one can imagine what an immense number of duplicates it had in its rather extensive vocabulary. If you were a Sumerian and wanted to render the sound *du*, which one of the twenty-three signs pronounced *du* would you choose? At the beginning the scribe did not know; almost any one would suffice. But this made for confusion. Some sort of agreement was more than necessary, and gradually one of the many signs representing the value *du* came to be used more and more frequently until in a later age it had practically a monopoly on that special sound. Also, in rendering words phonetically, it was quicker to use a symbol that represented a long word; that would save time. For instance, the Babylonian rendering of a foreign god's name, *Maruttash*, could be written *Marut-tash*, with two signs only. That was quick and effective and may be compared to our simplified spelling. But also it was a little uncertain because the sign for *Marut* could be read in different ways, and so could the sign for *tash*. One could take the chance of writing with two signs only in case there was no possibility of doubt about the reading. Here in America, if we abbreviate the name of a state into "Fla.," we read it "Florida"; but what about the man who does not know the names of the American states? So in many cases the scribes decided that it would be better to write down every word as fully as necessary. The very same name *Maruttash* is written in at least twenty different ways, beginning with the shortest that I have just mentioned and ending with the longest, which would be *Ma-ru-ut-ta-ash*. In between these two was the general writing practice of Babylonia. Wherever the scribe felt that the context was so clear that he could risk a short writing, he did so. When he was afraid that his signs might be misinterpreted, he used only those signs whose phonetic values were very simple and also well known.

From the very long spelling (*Ma-ru-ut-ta-ash*) of this name, the reader will already have discovered another fact about the writing of the Babylonians—that they did not develop an alphabet. Apart from the vowels, the best they could do was to write one vowel and one consonant, such as *ab* (or the reverse, *ba*), by means of one sign. Never by a single sign could they represent a single consonant. Hence the development of their writing was not carried to its logical conclusion.

Years ago, when speaking on this subject, I used to say that the Babylonians and Assyrians died too early—that is, that their civilization was cut off prematurely—so that they had no time for a complete development. I know better now. It is not that they did not know how to carry the development further but that they refused to make further changes in their system of writing. Anyone who has gone through the public schools of America or England knows what it is to learn the modern English spelling, with all the different ways of representing the same sounds, and with so many unnecessary letters which simply bewilder our children.

Why don't we change the English spelling? We refrain from doing so partly from conservatism, partly from the fear that we should be cutting ourselves off from our patrimony of the English language and literature. The advantages we all see, but we keep on spelling in the same old way. Exactly the same trouble confronted the Assyrians and Babylonians in the last centuries of their existence. They well knew that with a few changes they could develop an alphabet, for scribes using pen, ink, and foreign alphabets had come in from foreign countries. But the native scholars did not yield or give up their old traditions; they went down with colors flying. Is real history a *magistra vitae?* Does that mean we ought to learn how to simplify our spelling? Are we fools for resisting, or are we right for holding on? Perhaps one lesson is not enough, and in order to learn from history two lessons will be needed!

Chapter 6

AS HAS been said, writing on tablets was far from easy, and we cannot marvel that very few really attempted to master the practice. It was so much easier to hire someone to do the writing than to waste years at school one's self. The secretary, or personal scribe, became quite important and practically indispensable to all men transacting business. With the advent of typists in the present day, conditions appear to become more or less analogous, and, if our modern business leaders do not look out, they too may soon be unable to write!

So few were proficient in the "art of writing" that even kings boasted of the fact when they knew how to read and write. But this lack of proper training on the part of the large majority of the population did not stand in the way of their making an immense number of records covering all transactions. The law required that every business deal, even down to the smallest transaction, should be in writing and duly "signed" by the contracting parties and the witnesses. This was the law of 2000 B.C., and I may call to your attention the fact that it was not until two and one-half centuries ago that there was passed in England the "Statute of Frauds," which *requires* certain contracts to be in writing, a statute which has since been copied into the law of most of the states of our Union!

The signatures validating the document would have presented some difficulty if people had been really required to sign their names, but they got around the obstacle in a very simple way. Each man carried his signature around his neck! This was in the shape of a little cylinder of stone engraved with scenes from religious or social life. When the document was ready, each party

AN ANCIENT "SIGNATURE"—A CYLINDER SEAL AND ITS IMPRESSION

and witness would roll his cylinder over the wet clay, and the imprint which came out in relief served as his signature. Then the scribe would duly record the name of the man who had impressed his seal.

Just as in biblical times, most business was transacted near the gate of the city. There could always be found a crowd of people leisurely gossiping about local affairs or waiting for travelers bringing the latest news. There, as now, the public scribe would sit ready to sell his services when they were required. Instead of writing as we do by holding paper in one hand and pen in the other, he would simply have a small lump of clay and a piece of wood shaped into a stylus. The contracting parties arrive, come to a final understanding between themselves,

NATIVE DEALERS AND FOREIGN MERCHANTS COMPETE IN THIS BAGH-DAD MARKET

and explain to the scribe the nature of the transaction. After everything is clear, the scribe begins to write. His hands move very fast, turning the stick of wood or reed horizontally and vertically in rapid motions, and his tablet of clay is quickly covered with fine writing. The transacting parties—I imagine with a little misgiving because they could not read what was written down on the tablet —affixed their signatures, and the transaction was complete. In some cases a duplicate tablet was made so that both parties could have a document, but in most instances one tablet was sufficient.

The use of clay permitted an element of safety in writing important transactions that modern paper cannot give us. It is true, of course, that since the signs in the clay were merely impressed it would have been easy for

69

A MODERN IMITATION OF AN ANCIENT CLAY TABLET, INSCRIBED AND SEALED

the creditor, say, to scratch in an additional wedge or two; he might thereby alter the numerical figure or the meaning of a word just as can be done today by the man who "raises" a check by small additions or corrections. But this danger was often obviated by putting the document into a tamperproof envelope. The proceeding was very simple. After the tablet had been duly written and sometimes signed, the scribe would take in his hand a piece of clay and flatten it against a level surface, reducing it to the thickness of a piecrust. Then he would take the document and fold it into this sheet of clay. All the excess clay would be pinched off, leaving just enough to cover the document completely. Then the rough edges would be turned in and smoothed out with the result that the scribe had a tablet of exactly the same shape as the original, but slightly larger. On this he would proceed to write once more the same transaction in identical terms. On this cover the witnesses and contracting parties would again affix their seals—in fact, the seals on the envelope were much more important than the ones on the original document.

Many scholars have tried to explain how the scribe managed to prevent the envelope from sticking to the document inside. From the explanations there arose an argument which was very learned, and which paralleled the one in the Middle Ages as to why, if you put a live fish in a vessel completely full of water, the water does not overflow, but if you put in a dead fish, the water does overflow—an argument that went on for a long time until an enterprising soul did a little experimenting and found that the water overflowed in both cases! Exactly the same holds true in the case of envelopes. There was no necessity of first drying the tablet, or putting pulverized clay upon it so as to make it impossible for the envelope to adhere to the original document. It didn't in any case!

A document inclosed in an envelope was absolutely safe from being molested. If, in the future, discussion should arise concerning certain points, the transacting or disputing parties would go before the judge, and he would settle the case by simply tearing off the envelope. Since both the outside and the inside contracts were supposed to be exactly the same, any tampering with the envelope would immediately be discovered by looking at the original.

Further, no man could ever remove an envelope, change the original, and then replace the envelope, for the latter had to be destroyed before it could be removed. If he removed the envelope, altered the original, and then tried to put a new envelope on it, he would also have his troubles. First of all, he would have to procure the same witnesses, and, could he do so, he might just as well write an entirely new document. Second, clay shrinks considerably in drying, and the original tablet after a few days would become about one-fifth smaller than it was in its moist condition. A wet envelope on a preshrunk tablet, then, would never remain intact; since the envelope would begin to shrink and could not do so because the tablet inside was already dry and hard, it would have to crack. I have tried many times to put even a very thick envelope on a small hardened tablet, but the envelope invariably cracked. The result of all this is that the ancient writing medium, clay, assured not only for commercial but also for personal correspondence an inviolability which cannot be attained today. The man who knows the technique can always open a modern letter, no matter how many wax seals may have been put upon it to insure its safety.

As we said before, the law required written documents for every sort of business. When someone wanted to rent a house, he had to specify which house, what price, and from whom. A loan in money or a mortgage was, of course, duly recorded. Business men and exporting houses also made regular contracts with their agents and traveling salesmen. Employers clearly stipulated what their employees were to receive, and even brickmakers were bound by contracts to deliver their goods according to carefully written regulations and within a specified period of time. Careful regulations were likewise applied to

A CLAY TABLET IN ITS ENVELOPE

family affairs; and betrothals, marriages, wills, and testaments were matters to be properly recorded.

Since clay is imperishable, and most of these documents may be recovered some day, one may well imagine that a good percentage of the clay records found in Babylonia and Assyria are and will be more or less duplicates in content, presenting no especial interest. This however has given rise to a great misunderstanding. Once I read in an article that, after all, "We are not interested in the laundry lists of the ancient Sumerians." A little correction is necessary here. We never get laundry lists because the ancient Sumerians washed their dirty linen at home. But if we had them, they would be more than welcome. There are some subjects on which people rarely write, since they are generally taken for granted. As the Sumerians did not possess newspapers with full-page advertisements of great sales of mens' and ladies' garments, we are rather in the dark as to what they actually wore. This applies especially to all sorts of undergarments. While it might not be particularly enlightening to know anything of this kind, still a little information might be useful, especially if we wished to compare the costumes of one people with those of others living in different places.

But if we do not have laundry lists, we do have registers which resemble them closely, since some of the rich people in the land have preserved for us the lists of garments which they had to provide for the women of the household. While the names of some of the articles cannot be well understood, it certainly appears that ladies in those days spent just about as much on their personal wardrobes as do those of modern times!

But there is an entirely different consideration which sometimes makes the most unimportant looking document one of great scientific interest. Even when the pattern of the document is well known and does not call for any special comment, yet the personal names of the people mentioned may be quite significant. A pay roll which simply says, "One pound of bread to Mr. So-and-so," repeating it for different individuals twenty to fifty times, may be a most important document from a purely scientific standpoint. Reading the telephone directory cannot be said to be an occupation of absorbing interest; still, a scholar pondering over the telephone directories of the various cities in America could tell you immediately from the names themselves something about the mixture of population in the different cities. Comparing these directories one with another, he could follow a wave of migration from one coast to the other. He could tell us where it first started, when it ended, and in what parts of the country it settled. Movements of people are intensely interesting, and so even a list of pounds of bread delivered to different migrants can be called in some instances a scientific record of the first importance.

Necessarily, the old Babylonians and Assyrians had to have regular legal codes giving the rules which were to be followed. Several such codes have been found. Perhaps the one best known to the public at large is the code of Hammurabi, which has shown the world that the Babylonian mind was second to none and that the Romans, however much credit may be due to them, had been anticipated in this field by at least two thousand years. But there were also codes previous to that of Hammurabi; several kings tell us that they "established righteousness in the land," meaning that they codified existing laws.

One thing which needs to be stressed is that laws in ancient times were not invented and thought out by

THE LAW CODE OF HAMMURABI

some ingenious gentleman and afterward forced on the people. As a matter of fact, that cannot be done even now, and the state of affairs during prohibition was a splendid example of what happens when a law is imposed without the real consent of the people. Such consent expresses itself in the establishment of customs and self-imposed regulations which people would follow whether those regulations were on the lawbooks or not. They are a sort of law in themselves, although there are no penalties for their violation—a kind of gentleman's code or *noblesse oblige* which is just as strong as any active law. After such a regulation has already been observed, then it gets into the lawbooks, provided the legislature thinks it worth while.

Hammurabi tells us that he received his laws from the god of justice, and on the famous stele which contains his code he is pictured in the act of receiving instructions from the god. At the same time everyone in the land knew that the laws had not been dictated by the deity to the king, since most of them had already been in writing long before Hammurabi came into existence. What the people understood was that the god gave to Hammurabi sufficient wisdom to make a selection from the existing customs and to produce a code of law which would be acceptable and fair to all. And I must say that Hammurabi had a problem on his hands. The code has been criticized by some people who do not understand it because of its apparent contradictions or too severe penalties. The fact is that Hammurabi's immediate forbears came into the land of Babylonia at the head of only slightly civilized followers and planted themselves in the midst of a civilization which had absolutely nothing in common with their own. In Hammurabi's endeavor to codify existing customs, he had either to sanction or to reject practices that had arisen among two entirely different civilizations. On the one hand were his Semitic followers whose laws were based on the *lex talionis* just as the Hebrew laws were, and on the other were the interests of the highly civilized and, in the majority of cases, non-Semitic people. Throughout the code there is always the attempt to conciliate opposing interests without arousing too much hostility from either of the two groups. Also there is always the definite purpose of protecting the weak against the strong and making justice accessible to all. The more I read the code, the more I admire the intelligence and courage of the lawgiver.

This most important document was found in 1901 in the city of Susa in Iran (Persia). Originally it had been set up in a city of Babylonia in a place where it could be seen by the people, so that everyone who could read would know what his rights were under the law. An Elamite conqueror took away the big stele and erased part of it in order to substitute an inscription in his own honor—which, however, was never added. After this vandalism the stele remained in Susa until recovered in the twentieth century.

Here, again, for the erased portion of the code, the Babylonian tablets prove their value. For, of course, given the immense extent of the realm of Hammurabi, it would have been impossible for all the citizens to examine the stele itself whenever they wanted to consult the law. Consequently, many copies of the code had been made and deposited in various cities of the empire for the convenience of the people and the local lawyers. Fortunately for us, a tablet has been found in the city of Nippur containing several of the laws missing from the stele of Hammurabi. With time and a few more excavations the remaining gaps will certainly be filled.

The Assyrians also had a code of laws, but fate—by which we mean the spade of the excavator—has not so far given us the Assyrian code itself but only a series of amendments to the existing laws of 1350 B.C. or thereabouts concerning women. Compiled in a different stage of social evolution from the Hammurabi legislation, these laws give evidence of a different temperament and are somewhat harsher. A Hittite code of laws has also been found. Again in Hittite country the level of civilization was not so high as that of Babylonia, and, I am sorry to note, we get a very discouraging impression of moral conditions.

But with the discovery of the Babylonian, Assyrian, and Hittite codes we have not yet exhausted our possibilities. I hope and pray that we may some day secure another code which must have served the need of a large part of the population in pre- and early Assyrian times and which in form and practices must have been closer than any of the others to the Mosaic Code.

Chapter 7

RELIGION has always played a great part in the life of all peoples of antiquity. It permeated the daily life to an extent we can hardly realize at the present time. The kings not only reigned by divine right but they were also regarded as the actual representatives of gods and administered their kingdoms as vice-regents of the great gods. Therefore, he who was at the head of the state was both king and priest.

When one considers the great temples of ancient Mesopotamia, one must remember that they were not only the center of worship but also the heart through which pulsated the life of the community. Business, social, and intellectual activities were at home there. Attached to the temple was a school for scribes, and, as in the Middle Ages, the temple was also the center of science, especially of those branches which were closely interwoven with religion.

Temples also engaged in industry—in so far as the term can apply to the rather primitive conditions of those times in which each household manufactured practically everything necessary for daily life. Weaving, however, was taken up on a large scale, and we have pay rolls of weavers, mostly women, who received their daily wages from the temple. Women in industry are therefore no new problem.

MANUFACTURING AT HOME—THE COBBLER MAKING SHOES

Every important city had its great temple which carried on all these various activities because it enjoyed special privileges, just like a university today. It was exempt from taxes. Also, it received gifts, not so much from private citizens as from rulers who wanted thereby to win the favor of the gods. In view of this, it is no wonder that the temples acquired immense riches and became the centers not only of religious and intellectual pursuits but also of public life. Having large estates, they had to cultivate them and engage men to do the work; or lease or parcel them out and collect rent for them. Like banking institutions, they frequently loaned money, and at a good rate of interest. The ancient Babylonians, being good business men, did not consider that all interest was

81

A MODERN WEAVER IN IRAQ, HIS METHODS LITTLE CHANGED
THROUGHOUT THE CENTURIES

usury, as did the Hebrews, but they went a little bit too
far and commonly demanded 20 per cent—and occasionally as much as $33\frac{1}{3}$ per cent—of the capital as yearly
interest!

But the great temples did not have to rely on occasional
gifts and on the income they were able to make for themselves. They had a definite source of income in the "offerings" which were made by the people. Like the Hebrew tithe, these offerings had to be paid whether one
felt religiously impelled to do so or not. They were a
more or less fixed form of taxation which could well be

regarded as a steady income. Since in many cases the
temples, with their industrial and commercial activities,
were also the seat of government, where the real taxes
were collected, we have in ancient times a very good
parallel to the cry of "government in business" against
which so many people are now protesting. The taxes, or
offerings as they were really called, were paid mostly in
kind, since no coined money was then in circulation and
even pieces of silver would have been beyond the reach
of poor peasants.

We can now visualize the counting-room of one of the
big temples of ancient Babylonia. No row of typists
there, but certainly rows of scribes, either sitting or
squatting down beside little mounds of clay, busy check-

SETTING UP THE WARP FOR NEW CLOTH

AN ANCIENT SPINNER

ing and adding long accounts. The scribes would be mostly men, though women could be seen occasionally. It seems that the office girl made quite an early appearance, but was not much of a success.

Once when I was addressing a group of paper manufacturers, I humorously attempted to persuade them to abandon paper in favor of clay. I pointed out the cheapness of the material, its durability, and so on. But on one point I had to confess that the material I proposed failed completely. A tablet of clay, however big, dries out quickly, and must be written on all at one time, or very soon it cannot be written on at all. True, the old scribes must have attempted to cover the wet clay with a moist cloth, as does the modern sculptor when he wants to work for some time on a large amount of clay, but even this was a makeshift which could be used only in exceptional instances and with doubtful results. If you cannot have a book in which you can write when you wish, then of course a ledger in the modern sense of the word is an impossibility. This was one of the main difficulties with which ancient administrators were confronted. They solved it simply by writing on their ledgers all at one time.

The men who brought their offerings were given a receipt, and merely a memorandum of the affair was written down by the temple scribe and placed in a basket. At the end of a week those memos were taken out, the

A "MODERN" SPINNING WHEEL

AN EARLY BABYLONIAN PLOW AND GRAIN DRILL PORTRAYED
ON A CYLINDER SEAL

various offerings noted on them classified, and a ledger
tablet made to incorporate the totals. At the end of the
month, the weekly reports, in turn, were incorporated
in a monthly report, and at the end of the fiscal year
ledgers were written which summarized the totals obtained from the monthly reports. These yearly ledgers
were necessarily large tablets with many columns of
writing, and they closed with a series of totals for everything which had been included on the ledger. One would
end, for example, with "Total expenditures in wheat and
barley for the year such-and-such"; or another, "Total
receipts of cattle for the business year thus-and-so." Not
only the system of accounting, which was rendered difficult by the cumbersome material used for the writing,
but also the fact that payments were made in kind instead
of money must have greatly complicated the work of the
clerks. Obviously, one cannot add lambs and goats and

MODEL PLOW AND GRAIN DRILL, REPRODUCED FROM A SEAL IMPRESSION

measures of barley, even though they be received during the same day and for the same purpose. If the administrators of those times succeeded in keeping their accounts straight without an immense amount of red tape, they were made of better stuff than those we have at present!

In the course of excavation a large number of such provisional memos for taxes, for the week, the month, and the year, have been found. In one place nearly one hundred thousand were recovered at one time. Since their contents were not of very great interest to science, the

PLOWING IN IRAQ TODAY

A HUGE TABLET LEDGER—OF LITTLE COMMERCIAL VALUE THOUGH
FROM THE TIME OF ABRAHAM

museums and institutions of learning stopped acquiring them after they had what they considered a sufficient or representative number. The rest have been dispersed throughout the world by dealers who sold them to anyone who wanted them.

And here, perhaps, a word of warning will not be amiss. As may be easily understood, the commercial value of a Babylonian tablet is not at all in proportion to its size, beauty, or state of preservation. Some of the old ledgers are immense in size, yet the contents are not very important. Many of these temple records are dated about 2300 B.C., so that a dealer can truthfully recommend them as being older than Abraham, yet they are worth very little. The scientific and therefore the commercial value of a tablet is in direct ratio to its rarity and depends entirely on the content. People who want souvenirs should never pay high prices for things the value of which they cannot judge.

Chapter 8

UP TO a few years ago we knew all about ancient history. For ancient times the Bible was the main source, and the Hebrews held the stage. Peoples of Palestine and Syria, such as the Philistines, Amorites, Hittites, etc., were worthless barbarians who stood in the way of the people of God. It was therefore to be regretted that they had not been wiped out with the promptness which was to have been expected.

Of course, we knew about Egypt. First, it was mentioned in the Bible; and then its temples, the pyramids, and the Sphinx ever reminded us of the glory that was Egypt. Obviously, the land was the cradle of civilization.

The Babylonians also existed, and Nebuchadnezzar had to play the dangerous role of being the instrument of God for the punishment of the Hebrews. But, as a result of his actions toward Israel, was he not compelled, as a raving maniac, to eat of the grass of the field?

Then there were the Assyrians, who also played the part of God's scourge—a part for which they were extraordinarily well fitted. To historians of early times—and to many people of today—the Assyrians seemed ruthless military conquerors and nothing else.

Finally, said this version of ancient history, came the beginning of a new era with the rise of Greece. There the arts practically started, and philosophy began to interest mankind. A new civilization developed that was later transmitted to Rome and from Rome distributed to the rest of the world.

This outline of history was so simple, so thoroughgoing, and so eminently satisfactory that in some places it still holds its own and is taught to the younger generation. But all at once things began to happen. The Egyptian writings began to be deciphered and to tell a tale all their own. Great gaps in the outline began to be filled. Then came the turning-point; after a half-century more the Babylonian tablets began to tell their stories, and the result was a sweeping change in the reconstruction of the past. Documents of a historical character appeared in ever increasing numbers not only in the lands of Babylonia and Assyria but, as will be seen, in neighboring countries as well. We realize now that a large part of ancient history will have to be not only re-written but also completely reinterpreted.

What, now, can we learn of the political life of ancient times that will help us in our reinterpretation? A great deal; for, if every citizen had to record carefully each important transaction, we should expect the rulers to follow the common trend and preserve for future generations a complete story of their exploits. Compare the boasts of politicians and political parties today! We might say, in general, that no ancient Assyrian or Babylonian king ever took a chance that later generations might fail to know the good things he did. To insure his future prestige he went so far as to expose himself to the charge of being vainglorious.

If a king built a palace or restored a temple, he wrote the complete story of the undertaking and added to it a record of all his other pious deeds. This building inscription, as we call it, was generally written on a little barrel of clay, though sometimes more precious materials were used. Several copies of it were made and put in the cornerstone of the building being erected, exactly as we place books and records in the cornerstones of ours. In fact, the practice is so well known that archeologists never fail to look for these foundation boxes because the records contained in them will give interesting information concerning the building in question.

But the king did not stop here in his precautions against losing the credit he thought he was entitled to receive. Where baked bricks were used in the construction, they were stamped with an inscription that read somewhat like this: "The temple of the god So-and-so, built by King So-and-so, the great king, the king of Sumer and Akkad." Such temple records are very common wherever excavation is conducted in a royal city or in a city containing temples that were worthy of the king's attention. Archeologists find so many of them that, after a few specimens have been obtained for the museums, the others are thrown into the dump.

While I was watching the excavation at Ur of the Chaldees, Sir Leonard Woolley, who was in charge of the work, gave orders to the laborers to preserve carefully all inscribed bricks so that they could be examined. If the inscription proved to be either new or interesting, the brick was taken from the workman and he was given a tip, amounting to about four cents. Of course, the workmen were very careful to keep all such bricks and to insist on an examination of their finds. Now one early king of the city of Ur, called Ur-Nammu, had done a considerable amount of building, but for the many bricks that carried his name he had used a formula that was practically stereotyped. Consequently, bricks with his stamp were worthless and never brought a tip to the workmen; while we were going around glancing at inscriptions, in almost every case we had to say, "Ur-Nammu," which, translated to the workmen's point of view, simply meant "No tip." It was interesting to observe the reactions of those laborers. They called Ur-Nammu a variety of names that cannot be repeated here! The king would have been very much astonished had he been able to realize what kind of praise later generations gave him for his labors.

But, as has been said before, most of the great buildings of ancient Babylonia were erected with sun-dried bricks. Obviously, on such a brick, which was set in a mortar made of mud, no inscription would ever show. So the kings thought of another system. They wrote the same inscription that they would have placed on clay bricks, or an abridgment of it, on little clay nails. These were baked and stuck into the walls just underneath the mortar at intervals of about one meter. Any later king who demolished those walls would find the nails, and there could never be any doubt that the temple in question had been either built or repaired by one of his predecessors.

Of course, all these precautions had not in view the archeologists of three or four thousand years later, but

AN ANCIENT DOG LEFT HIS FOOTPRINTS ON THIS STAMPED
BRICK

one can easily imagine how welcome these inscriptions in
the cornerstones or at the base of the walls or within the
walls themselves are to modern scholars. They render
unnecessary complicated studies, the results of which
would always be more or less uncertain. We can easily
reconstruct the fortunes of a city by observing when its
buildings fell into ruins or by whom they were restored.
We may even follow the vicissitudes of a special god by
ascertaining when his temple was built or reconstructed.
We have in some of the walls of the temples a stratification
as clear as that in geological formations, with the additional help that each stratum contains definite indication

94

SO PROUD OF HIS DRAINAGE SYSTEM WAS AN EARLY SOVER-
EIGN THAT HE BUILT IT WITH STAMPED BRICKS

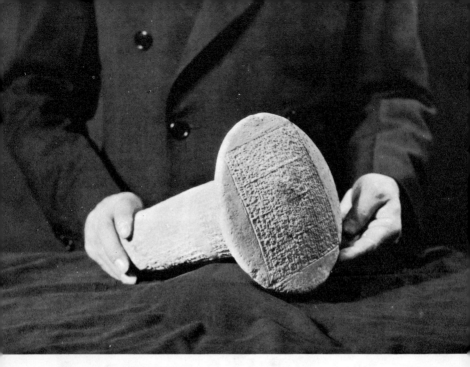

AN INSCRIBED CLAY "NAIL"

of its date. For the foregoing reasons we are quite willing to forgive the ancient kings for their apparent lack of modesty.

We are also grateful to them for the complete records they give of their campaigns and activities. These are recorded on hollow polygons of clay with six, seven, or eight faces, each covered with as much writing as it could possibly hold. Sometimes cylinders of clay, also hollow, contain in three or four columns the same inscription. These too were manufactured in large numbers, and I am certain the work of the royal scribes must have been extremely monotonous, since they had to copy over and over the very same inscription. These big polygons or cylinders were also built into the cornerstones of the royal palaces to commemorate the mighty deeds of the rulers; and copies of them were also retained in the royal libraries. For some kings we already have all the information we can desire; for the complete record of others we shall have to wait until excavators hit upon the right buildings.

The only trouble with these royal inscriptions is that they do not always tell us what we want to know. It is natural and understandable that the ancient sovereigns should try to present themselves in the best possible light. In a country like Assyria, surrounded by mountains occupied by enemies ready to swoop down upon the unprotected plains, a king would be likely to boast of his prowess in battle and of the fact that he had so frightened the

CLAY "NAILS" IN PLACE

surrounding enemies that the land could develop in peace. Hence the Assyrian records are tales of battles. Actually we know that some of the kings were no soldiers at all; one of them who styles himself as a great warrior has actually been accused of cowardice! On the other hand, it is only incidentally and rarely that we find Assyrian kings telling us of the libraries they established, the canals they built, and the immense pains they took for the welfare of their people. We do know, however, of a revival of interest in literature at the time of Sargon, although it was he who destroyed Samaria, deported part of the original population, and refilled the city with peoples taken from different parts of the empire. We can

CLAY PRISM OF SENNACHERIB (*left*) AND BARRELS OF SARGON (*center*) AND NEBUCHADNEZZAR (*right*)

UNCOVERING A FOUNDATION RECORD

now see that this Sargon was a patron of the arts, and yet he was primarily responsible for the "Samaritan" problem and for kindling the hatreds that continued down to the beginning of the Christian Era so that it took all Christ's courage to defy conventions and actually enter into conversation with a woman from the despised city!

Conversely, in another land safer from invasion, military virtues were not at all stressed. And so we have Nebuchadnezzar, a great king and a great conqueror, who passes over in complete silence all of his splendid military exploits and spends his time telling us how many temples he built and repaired and what special grants

99

A LION FROM THE ISHTAR GATE OF NEBUCHADNEZZAR AT BABYLON

he made to the shrines of the gods. His ambition seems to have been to leave to posterity a record for piety.

Furthermore, the records are reliable only up to a certain point. You cannot expect a man to consume his time and money in telling the world that he has been defeated. Let the enemy do that! He will talk about his own victories, or relate his story in such a way that a defeat will seem to have been a victory. Here a study of the maps will suffice to fill in some of the obvious gaps and to reconstruct the facts. If the first battle of a Chicago king is "won" at New York, the second at Philadelphia, and the fifth at Pittsburgh, it is quite evident that the army is really retreating. The leader does not dare to tell the truth. If "half" the opposing army is destroyed in the first battle, an equal amount in the third, a large number in the fourth, and there are still enough enemies left to keep the king out campaigning, obviously there is misrepresentation somewhere!

And yet understatements, misstatements, and evident falsehoods do not destroy the scientific value of royal inscriptions. All of them must be interpreted by men who realize the inherent difficulties and dangers, but that is nothing new, and this work is now being done. And as we look round about us, on statesmen, presidents, dictators and their pronouncements, all we can say is that the old Assyrians and Babylonians wrote their history in exactly the same way as we do now!

In antiquity, time reckoning did not begin with some important event as it does today, when we count from the approximate date of the birth of Christ. The ancients obviously knew nothing of 5 A.D. or 1055 B.C. Instead, a year took its name from a significant happening of the same year or of the year before. Thus we have "Year in which the great temple of Marduk in the city of Babylon was built," or "Year in which King So-and-so defeated the armies of So-and-so," or "Year in which the royal canal was dug." Obviously, no one could remember all of these dates unless he had some help. Consequently, the scribes drew up lists of the date formulas of each king, and so we have the list giving us the year-names of Hammurabi: first, "The year Hammurabi became king"; second, "The year Hammurabi made the throne for the god of Babylon"; and so on, continuing through the thirty-first year in which he became ruler of all Babylonia up to the forty-third year and his death. We thus get not only the number of years which a king reigned, but also the sequence of the most important events which occurred during his rule.

ASSYRIANS MOVING A BULL COLOSSUS INTO POSITION (DRAWN FROM A RELIEF)

Such lists of date formulas were also supplemented by lists of the kings. In these, the different dynasties were placed one after another, and all the kings in each dynasty with the years of their reigns were carefully included. It is difficult to overestimate the historical importance of such lists for the reconstruction of ancient events in the Orient. But, while the lists are reliable so far as years of reigns and names of kings within each dynasty are concerned, they are untrustworthy in this— that they place one after another dynasties that were practically contemporaneous and therefore overlapping. Hence we know that we cannot add the totals of each dynasty and reach the date for some of the earliest ones.

Also, while the years of the reign of each king are correct for historical times, they become absolutely incredible when we reach a high antiquity. Some of the early half-mythical kings have been given as many as seventy-two thousand years of reigning! In this we have a close parallel to the long lives of the Hebrew patriarchs. But while it is useless to try to compare the names of the early mythical kings of Babylonia with those of the patriarchs, something may still be gained from an examination of the two records and the numbers involved. It is also folly to try to surmount the difficulty presented by these large numbers by imagining that each year of the earliest patriarchs was shorter than ours, and that therefore the life of Methuselah would not be more than the usual three score and ten. If we do that to Methuselah, who is said to have lived nine hundred and sixty-nine years, what

THE ORIENTAL INSTITUTE'S "CHERUB" AS DISCOVERED BY THE AUTHOR (*see* Frontispiece)

would happen to a king who reigned seventy-two thousand years? Obviously, we cannot believe that both Babylonians and Hebrews would always so precisely call a few days a year.

A much quicker way out of the difficulty is this: Hebrew historians who tried to bridge the gap between what they thought was the correct date for the creation of the world and the time for which they had sufficiently reliable records, found that they had only a limited number of names to do it with. Rather than invent new ones, they simply stretched the lives of the ones they had to fill their need. Now the Hebrews could not imagine that their early heroes could be so very far removed, and they set for them a comparatively recent date. But the Babylonians of any one generation, surrounded on all sides by monuments infinitely older than they themselves, knew better and gauged much more accurately. They too stretched the few personages they had to fill the gaps, but of course they had to stretch them a great deal more. Here, again, we see that it is a mistake to reject the very early dynastic lists as completely untrustworthy because of the long span of life attributed to the heroes. It is much better to try to understand what prompted such an action and use the information which has been transmitted to us for what it may be worth.

To the kings' personal records found buried in the walls of the ancient buildings, to the date formulas, and to the king lists, we can also add as a good source of information the actual correspondence which the kings carried on with their officials, instructing them as to what they should do in difficult cases. In this correspondence we see the king really at the helm, trying to govern in most instances according to the best of his ability; and, incidentally, we get also a complete picture of the condition of his subjects.

Chapter 9

THE people in Babylonia and Assyria, just like all other ancient peoples the world over, had their own family worship. The father was the high priest, and little clay figurines of the gods and small replicas of the houses of these gods were part and parcel of every household. Offerings were presented to them, and devotions restricted to the immediate members of the household were held at stated intervals. There is no question but that these family gods, who were considered the guardian angels of the family fortunes, received a large share of worship. The great gods of the pantheon, whose business it was to protect the whole state and who were worshiped in the temples, were too lofty and too important to take good care of the individual worshipers. To be sure, one went to the temple as a matter of duty and also because one felt that it was better to be on the good side of those very important personages!

It would be fascinating if we could have a complete picture of this family worship. Unfortunately, we can gather only glimpses of it from the family contracts. A mother may divide among her children the little houses of the gods, describing each one and also commenting on its condition. In his will the father may leave his household gods to the eldest son, cautioning him, however, that he must allow the other children to come to the house

THE MOTHER-GODDESS, MOST UNIVERSALLY AND
FERVENTLY ADORED OF DEITIES

ON THIS ALTAR IN A PRIVATE HOME WERE OFFERED FAMILY SACRIFICES

and bring their offerings. Evidently the family devotion had to be carried on in the same way as before. Since worship of these gods was restricted to the immediate family, admission to such worship was proof that one was officially accepted as an actual member of the family with all the duties and privileges which this membership involved.

The Babylonian tablets give also a very welcome light on some biblical episodes. Everyone remembers how Rachel stole the teraphim or family gods of her father. When the theft was discovered, the whole party was so minutely searched that Rachel barely succeeded in sav-

ing her loot through an ingenious strateg
should one go to so much trouble for a coupl
terra cotta figurines that might not be worth two
The tablets give the reason: if a son-in-law possessed th
household gods of his father-in-law, then he was considered a real son and shared in the inheritance. By stealing
the family gods, Rachel expected to make her husband an
immediate member of her father's household and, consequently, one who could rightfully claim a portion of her
father's inheritance. It was not a question of two figurines
but of a large share of property.

Though we cannot at present reconstruct in detail the
family worship because up to the present time references
to it are but casual, we can form a clear idea of what the

A WALL NICHE FOR THE IMAGE OF A HOUSEHOLD GOD

The religious literature of Baby-
... large and so varied in character as
... We have psalms and litanies in
... nd even of the deified kings. Some of
... to be sung in the temples and were
... sitions telling what the priests or the
... o. A number of the psalms also indicate
... strument to be used. Many are the stories
of the g... ods and the epics of the semidivine heroes of
antiquity. Creation stories, ancient cosmogonies, and
myths—many with a good philosophical substratum—
have also been recovered.

It is strange to notice that practically all the existing
literature was put down in written form a century or two
after 2000 B.C.—a very difficult time from a political
standpoint. The peaceful Sumerian people had been
completely conquered by the less civilized but, in a military sense, stronger Amorite invaders. Hammurabi had
made short work of the many city-states and had founded
an immense kingdom. A great administrator, he tried to
unify his empire by giving laws and also by making his
own Semitic language the official one throughout his
dominions. That was a deathblow to the ancient Sumerian civilization. And while we cannot but feel sorry
at present over the collapse of one of the greatest cultures
of ancient times, yet I am sure that credit is due Hammurabi for realizing at least that the damage was done.
He knew that the Sumerian language was good and that
his followers could not afford to lose its great intellectual
gifts, but he knew also that it was dying. Whether
prompted by the king himself or by the vanishing

110

scholars of Sumerian, a great desire seems to have taken hold of everyone to put down in writing everything which he thought should be preserved for posterity. Up to that point wandering musicians had kept alive most of the psalms and sagas. But if this older tradition were to continue to be nurtured even though the Sumerians were being denationalized, at least the civilization could be saved. It so happens that the deathblow to Sumerian civilization was also the signal for the rise of great literary activity. The temple schools and libraries of ancient Babylonia became filled with literary productions of the most varied character. How long after this the bards continued to go from house to house, singing their songs and entertaining the people in exchange for gifts and the plaudits of their listeners, we have no means of knowing. But at least we know that some of them got their names "in print" who otherwise would never have had the chance. At the bottom of some of these songs the scribe has written "from the mouth of Mr. So-and-so." This explains why the very same story recorded in different places sometimes presents considerable variation. A good deal of it is owing to the great imaginative power of the singer, who could add touches of his own to the age-old theme.

The state of affairs described above presents some troubles to one who wishes to interpret the religious literature. We know that none of these songs is much later than 2000 B.C. The old scribes apparently did well in preserving what they had, because no important addition appears to have been made in nearly two millenniums after that time. Even in the case of Assyrian stories, or what we once thought to be Assyrian stories, ancient

A MINSTREL AND HIS HARP

ANOTHER EARLY MUSICIAN

DISSONANT TO WESTERN EARS IS THE MUSIC OF THIS MODERN
ORIENTAL ORCHESTRA

libraries are beginning to yield the old Sumerian origi-
nals. But, while we know that they were *written down*
by 1900, how much older actually are they? Some of
them had doubtless circulated by word of mouth for
many centuries. Others are certainly more recent and
date about the time when they were put down in writing.
But every story must be dated from its own internal evidence, since there is no rule that will apply to all.

Moreover, the stories have been edited. Doubtless
those episodes or editions which did not conform to the
ideas of the listeners were dropped. The exploits of a
local god would tend to receive more emphasis in the city
where that deity was worshiped. This is human, and the

113

vaudeville performer of our day, if he is intelligent, always changes his skit to some extent according to the place where it is given. Fortunately for us, here again we get copies from different cities of psalms sung by different bards. It is for us to decide what features are essential and which ones are subject to more or less change.

But the work of piecing together this religious literature is far from easy. In the question of a business transaction

TYPICAL OF THE TEMPLE CULT IS THIS SCENE

Assyriologists have no trouble at all. Each contract is a complete unit, sufficiently intelligible in itself and still clearer when compared with countless other documents which follow the same general pattern. In the case of royal annals the name of a king, a geographical name, or a reference to a well-known event will quickly furnish a clue, and an inscription can easily be placed in its proper background. But in religious literature no such distinguishing features exist. First of all, as there is no clean-cut division between the different types of texts, a psalm may be lyric in some places and dragged down to monotonous litany in others. A song in honor of a god

114

may recount his exploits and merge with myths and cosmogonies. An old myth, with very few changes, may be made to honor the local king and actually to appear as a new creation. Often in reading a particular psalm one has recollections of others, just as when hearing some very modern music one can recognize motifs and excerpts from older and almost forgotten melodies.

Moreover, very long literary works naturally had to be written on a number of tablets, and we might have difficulty arranging these in their proper order. But in such cases the old scribes tried to make their own and incidentally our task easier. At the bottom of each tablet they wrote, "Tablet X of series so-and-so," and then added the opening lines of the following tablet. Through these notations they could place the tablets next to one another on the shelves just as we keep our books today.

Unfortunately for us, we do not get the tablets from the library shelves. Not only have the tablets themselves in many instances been broken into pieces but the whole library also is now in wild confusion. The discoverer of today who plans to reconstruct the ancient literature of Babylonia and Assyria has before him a jigsaw puzzle of the first magnitude. He must examine each fragment by itself and from its contents try to determine where it belongs. Then he must hunt up the published material of the special group and see whether the new fragment adds anything new or fits into some previous break. It is as if all the books of the Latin writers had been torn first into pages and then most of the pages into small fragments, and the whole accumulation of torn pieces of paper thoroughly mixed up and only a handful of them given to someone who has to reconstruct them into a whole. Of course, he wouldn't mix up the *Aeneid*, but how many portions of Caesar's writings would he attribute to some other author?

Still, the work is not so hopeless as it may appear. If a modern book is important, if it is a best seller, many editions of it are published. If an ancient epic or psalm

THE MIGHTY GILGAMESH REPRESENTED ON A SEAL IMPRESSION

was significant, many copies of it were made in many cities. If a section of it is missing from the collection in the Oriental Institute of the University of Chicago, it may be found tomorrow in Philadelphia, or London, or Berlin. With a little time and a considerable amount of patience, all the important elements of this venerable literature will be pieced together. What we shall miss, let us say a hundred years from now, will be a good many of the songs which had only local importance, and here and there a few lines or perhaps a "page" or "half-page" from some of the great epics. Just as today the discovery

116

of a few verses which have been lost from any of the books of the New Testament would cause widespread interest in the learned world, so perhaps a century or two from now some orientalist will attract the attention of scholars by announcing that a new tablet discovered by him has finally closed the last remaining gap in the famous Gilgamesh epic. We cannot hope for that today. Our work is that of the pioneer, and, if we can add to the general knowledge of the literature to any considerable extent, we are satisfied, even though many gaps still remain. Even at this very early stage some of the short stories are complete, being pieced together from fragments now scattered in various museums all over the world. Once I had even greater luck. At the University of Pennsylvania I had studied one part of a medical text. Some time later during a visit to the museum at Constantinople I discovered the other part, not from another edition but from the very same tablet!

Chapter 10

IT IS very unusual if after a talk on Babylonian literature someone in the audience does not ask this question: "Do the cuneiform texts prove or disprove the Bible?" As one can easily surmise, it is impossible to answer that question with "yes" or "no." We ought to do a great deal of thinking and try to define the question very clearly before we attempt even the beginning of an answer. The Bible is not a book but a series of books, written by different authors at different periods. It is not confined to a single subject and, while it is chiefly a religious book, it also contains history, cosmogonies, poetry, philosophy, and other types of writing.

Let us take the subjects in order—first, the historical record. The Bible tells us that the Assyrians captured Samaria. Cuneiform texts tell us the same thing. Again, the Bible declares that, when Sennacherib tried to conquer Jerusalem, Jehovah protected the city, and the invader's army was destroyed through divine intervention. From his own accounts we know that Sennacherib did try to take Jerusalem, but he does not claim to have succeeded in doing so. Hence, in both these cases, one may say that the texts corroborate the Bible, though some people may wish to state it the other way and say that the Bible corroborates the cuneiform texts. There are no objections to either point of view.

On the other hand, the Assyrian king Shalmaneser on his Black Obelisk presents a picture of Jehu paying him homage and bringing him presents. That episode is not in the Bible. Shall we therefore say that the Bible is not true? Of course, the correct interpretation is that Jehu avoided mentioning a day of humiliation; and, even had he mentioned it, some patriotic follower would have seen to it that the reference to an unfortunate episode did not remain in the accounts. The fact is that all these verifications—or lack of them—of reported events are quite secondary. The Bible is a religious book, and history plays quite a minor part in it. Moreover, most of this late history is known to be correct and does not need to be verified. Let us leave for the time being late historical accounts and pass to something more interesting, such as myths and cosmogonies.

To start from the beginning, let us take the creation story in the first chapter of the Bible. In almost every book dealing with the subject, this story is immediately compared with the Assyrian creation narrative, and deductions are made. A considerable amount of erudition and ingenuity is generally expended on the work, and finally the responses will come in more or less these words: "The similarities found are not sufficient to suggest either direct borrowing or direct relationship." And this settles the problem to the satisfaction of many inquirers. But the procedure, simple and effective though it may be, takes too much for granted.

The Bible does not give us one creation story but several of them; the one which happens to be featured in chapter 1 of Genesis appears to be the one which had the least

THE OBELISK OF SHALMANESER

vogue among the common people. It stands alone at the very beginning of the Holy Book, and it represents the highest development of Hebrew theological thought. Its conceptions are so beautiful and so lofty as to give it a place by itself, although creation stories in other books of the Bible are completely at variance with it. The "Assyrian story," which is generally compared with it, is not Assyrian at all but goes back thousands of years into the earliest Sumerian times. It happens to have become the "Assyrian" story because it was the first creation account discovered and because it was written in Assyrian, a language easily understood, instead of in Sumerian, which still presents many difficulties of interpretation. Thus the twofold advantage of early discovery and easy interpretation made that special account the "Assyrian story of creation." We can say in its favor that it must have been a very popular story to have survived thousands of years, to have traveled from ancient Sumer to the city of Nineveh, and even to have been translated into a different language. That it deserved the popularity it enjoyed there can be no doubt. It is dramatic, has plenty of action, and fully explains what it intends to explain.

The opposite is true of Genesis, chapter 1. That certainly contains the more beautiful concepts, and it does reflect a very high state of theological development. Nevertheless, it is merely an enumeration of facts, and the style is stilted and monotonous. It was evidently produced in scholarly circles and of necessity condemned to remain there, or the general public would have known it. If we wish to compare that kind of scholarly presentation with a cuneiform narrative, we must compare it with

THE MOUND OF BABYLON

another type of story than the "Assyrian" story. It is useless to hope to get results by comparing a page from a
book of philosophy with a drama born out of the passions
and emotions of daily life. Sumerian parallels to the
story in the first chapter of Genesis so far have been found
only in a very fragmentary state. A complete narrative
may or may not be found in the near future; but, if we
find it within a reasonably short time, it will be mere
luck, because that type of story will have enjoyed as little
popularity in Sumer as it did among the Hebrews. But,
by all means, let us stop wasting time in endeavoring to
compare narratives which do not admit of comparison,
and let us begin our research from another angle.

Although the Hebrew theologians rejected the Babylonian type of story as being far below the conceptions of
their god, the people in general did not seem to think so.
While Genesis, chapter 1, still remains isolated in its
high conceptions, throughout other books of the Bible
we get many echoes of Jehovah's famous fight against the
monster Leviathan. Rejected or not by theologians, this
was certainly the popular creation story of the common
people. If that is so, a brief résumé of this exceedingly

popular creation myth as it was understood in Babylonia may be of interest here. I am sorry the limits of this little book make it impossible for me to reproduce the beautiful poetic form of the original.

Before heaven and earth had been created, that is, at the very beginning, the whole universe was an immense watery chaos. Out of this terrible confusion primitive divine beings came into existence, though they themselves were as yet so chaotic in appearance that they could not even be described. Ages passed, and the gods began to take tangible shape and to act. A group of them decided to bring some sort of law and order into the chaos. This was a very bold step which aroused the sharp antagonism of the more conservative deities who thought the old state

THE TOWER OF BABEL—A MODERN RECONSTRUCTION

of affairs was good enough and should be continued. Especially was their decision resented by Tiamat, the mother of chaos, a female deity in the form of a dragon personifying the worst, or best, features of it.

When Tiamat heard of the gods' intentions to bring order into her own domain and thereby diminish not only her authority but also her well-being, she decided that it was time to fight. Out of the chaos which she embodied she created immense demons comprising parts of various animals and possessing horrible powers of destruction. She called together her husband and her newly created army and prepared for the fray. At first the gods were frightened. The task they had undertaken threatened to be more than they had bargained for, but finally one deity advanced to battle. He gripped his weapons and commanded the four mighty winds to stand by. Tiamat, the personification of chaos, came forward and opened her mouth wide. This gave the god his chance. Immediately he threw into her mouth the mighty winds; they pushed so hard that the body of the dragon goddess became so swollen she could hardly move. The god thereupon finished her with his weapons. Then a question arose: What should he do with the gigantic carcass? It must have been immense in size, and in form it must have resembled that of a huge flat vase. After mature deliberation, the god split the body open. One portion he laid flat, and it became the earth. The other half he bent over the earth, and it became the heavens. Chaos was dead. The work of establishing order in the universe could now begin. Tiamat's husband, a very minor being, had also been captured in battle. The gods beheaded him, and from the blood that came out of his body, mixed with the clay of the soil, they created mankind. This is why we men have something of the divine in us, however difficult it may be to find it.

As mentioned above, it is impossible to say when the story originated and who was the first god to be created with the gift of transcendent might. Beyond the shadow of a doubt he must have been Sumerian, and one can imagine in this important role either the great god Enlil, one of the most prominent of the ancient pantheon, or perhaps the warrior Ninurta. Centuries passed, and the power of the Sumerians came to an abrupt end with the rise of Babylon under Hammurabi. Marduk, the new god of this rather new city, certainly had no right to appropriate to himself the glory of so great a deed. He was a baby among the gods, and his city had not even been in existence when the mighty feat was accomplished. But in Hammurabi's time Babylon was the center of the kingdom. Young or not, Marduk, backed by Hammurabi's armies, could now claim to be the most important god in the land. He lacked a patent of nobility, but that was given him by the theologians of the time. The famous old story was taken up again and given certain touches so that it would fit the new conditions.

When the monster Tiamat came, we are told, the gods were frightened. None of the old gods whose duty it was to take up the defense of the pantheon could muster enough courage to advance against the enemy. Finally, after all the other deities had failed to do so, young Marduk, the god of Babylon, presented himself. Of course, he was not fit for the battle. He was too young; he knew too little; he had too little power. But the emergency was there and the fate of the gods hung in the balance, so the old gods gratefully accepted Marduk as the rescuer. They endowed him with all the powers in their possession, and thus enabled him to meet the enemy on even terms. He received wisdom, strength, and all the other virtues which had been the property of older and more mature gods. Thus equipped he went into the fray and won. By

THE GOD MARDUK

the victory, on the one hand, and by the special powers which he had acquired and which remained with him, on the other, he was naturally fitted for the new role of head of the pantheon. Hence the old leader was deposed, and Marduk took his place.

Centuries passed, and the power of Babylon declined. More to the north a strong Assyrian empire demanded recognition. The armies of Ashur marched forth to victory after victory. Presently the old problem of Tiamat again emerged. The Assyrians asked why should not their god, Ashur, be the one who had fought the terrible battle? To be sure, the Assyrians were less subtle than the Babylonians and did not use the finesse that Hammurabi's theologians had employed. Like Napoleon, who decided he did not need to be crowned according to the rules and crowned himself without further ado, so the Assyrian priests gave the honor to Ashur simply by taking the old Babylonian tablets and recopying them, substituting the name of their own god for that of Marduk. The work was not very carefully done, and in some places the name of Marduk still creeps in. But in view of the present power of Ashur, who could doubt that he had slain the dragon?

This story traveled beyond the limits of Mesopotamia into Palestine; but even the powerless Hebrews would never think of accepting a foreign god to symbolize the beginning of creation. Whether the priests liked it or not, the common people in their religious verses celebrated Jehovah as the slayer of the Leviathan or dragon. In time the Hebrew books were incorporated with those of Christianity. Christians did not look with favor upon the

THE GOD ASHUR EMERGES FROM THE WINGED SUN DISK IN THIS SYM-
BOLIC REPRESENTATION

idea that Jehovah should be regarded as the performer
of a deed that suited better the character of the nearer
and more modern centuries. So St. George slew the
dragon.

Today we are stressing the strange phenomenon that in
the minds of the people in general the importance and
motivating influence of religion are slowly being under-
mined by an increasing emphasis on the discoveries of
science. Personally, I cannot say that I approve of the
change of emphasis, but the fact remains that it is taking
place under our very eyes. A few years ago one of the
great American universities decided to honor its presi-

dent, a celebrated scientist, by erecting a statue of him on the campus while he was still alive. The statue was duly unveiled, and there under the left foot of the scientist was an overgrown lizard being crushed to death. I wonder if that excellent scholar ever thought what it all meant. Of course, it represented science destroying the bad influence of ignorance. But did the scientist realize that he was the direct successor of Enlil, Marduk, Ashur, Jehovah, and St. George? As I was contemplating that statue, a thought passed through my mind: who will fight the dragon next? If I could give the answer, I could also tell what direction human civilization will take in the next thousand years.

Now let us go back to the question with which we started. A scientific comparison of the myth contained in

ANOTHER SYMBOL OF ASHUR

the first chapter of Genesis with that in Babylonia has not yet been made for the very simple reason that too little is known about the Babylonian myths. Before science can give any sort of definite verdict, it will have to wait for the results both of excavation and of laborious decipherment and translation of the texts that have already been obtained. But even if we should be able to prove an absolute parallel, a definite answer could not be given. An example will show this. Out of the literature of Babylonia and Assyria has come a deluge story which certainly parallels that of the Bible. We have the well-known ark, covered with bitumen—just like the one in the Bible—and in it one particular man with his family, warned by the gods of an approaching deluge. Rains inundate the earth and kill off the population, the ark lands on a mountain, the man sends out three birds, the rescued come out and offer a sacrifice. The similarities are so striking that everyone agrees that the stories are the same.

Of course there are some differences. The Babylonian story, being cast against a polytheistic background, has many gods among the actors. One of them decides upon the deluge, and another betrays the secret. A rough but vivid feature in the Babylonian story is the notion that the gods themselves, after the deluge had been unloosed on the earth, became frightened by it. We could never imagine Jehovah in that role. But poetical and polytheistic though the story may be, still it has a touch lacking in the biblical story; and Ishtar, the goddess of love, confronting the great god who was chiefly responsible for the deluge, reproaches him most bitterly for his crime.

130

The god, she proclaims, had no right to destroy all mankind; some of the men might have been bad, but there were also good ones among them. If the men had sinned, the god could have sent a famine to punish them, or he might have sent lions to diminish their number, but a general flood should never have been sent. And this de-

THE GODDESS ISHTAR

nunciation ends with a sentence that reaches a height never approached by the Old Testament, "On the sinner lay his sin," which simply means that each man is responsible only for his own actions. The Hebrews never understood the truth of this.

But apart from differences, the two stories are undoubtedly the same. Does this, then, prove the Bible?

131

Yes, some will say, it is an undeniable confirmation that the deluge actually did occur. No, others will say, it is an absolute proof that Hebrew myths came from Babylonia. And there we are. The answer to the question will be given by each one of us according to his own background and religious and scientific training.

There is one thing Babylonian literature does do for the Bible—it makes it more understandable. We must remember that the Old Testament is practically all that we have of the ancient Hebrew language. Hence many words occur only once or twice and cannot be understood from their context. Babylonian and Assyrian literature, immensely rich in texts of all kinds, is written, for the most part, in a language which belongs to the same Semitic group as Hebrew. Further, the very same words and expressions which are not understandable in Hebrew are often quite clear in the Babylonian texts.

But something must still be added. It is not only a question of getting a clearer idea about meanings of words or of phrases. In the Hebrew Bible we have too little to give us a complete picture. It is just as if we had in front of us a great panel richly covered with frescoes. Here and there on different portions of the panel some figures stand out, perfectly preserved and clear in all detail, but there are blank spaces between these figures, and, unless we can fill in the gaps, we cannot understand the meaning or purpose of the figures. The relationship which should bind them together is lacking. But Babylonian and Assyrian literature has such a complete background. We understand the picture because we can fit in the missing portions.

Furthermore, no scholar doubts that in the process of copying and recopying and editing and re-editing portions of the ancient books, new facts were discovered and added. This does not mean that anyone infringed upon the "copyrighted" work of another. Professor Jastrow used to say that there was this difference between an oriental book and one of our books: In our times a book is first completed, then released, and then it begins to live; in the ancient Orient, as soon as a book was completed, its life was ended. So long as the topic of the book interested people, it was read, copied again, supplemented, and passed along to be improved—or perhaps spoiled—by the next reader. After interest in the subject had died down, no one cared to read it any more, and the book was completed—dead. There was no idea in those times of authorship and no fear of intruding on someone else's property. A book was nobody's property. It belonged to everyone.

In the case of the Bible, besides this process of expansion that belongs to all literary productions of antiquity, there was another and contrary trend, namely, the jealous censorship on the part of the priest, who did not want the book to contain episodes or explanations which might not agree with his own conception either of the god or of what was fit to be incorporated into the history of the founders of the race, and who piously but nonetheless ruthlessly eliminated what he did not approve. This constant process of "improving" has left the Bible a book which is very much alive but also has made difficult the task of scholars who wish to use it as a source in tracing the development of ideas or institutions. And again the

Babylonian texts turn out to be useful. We get the first, the later, and the final copies of ancient documents, so that a scientific and comparative study of such a subject as sacrifice will lack nothing.

Finally, Christian peoples formerly examined passages of the Bible wholly apart from their oriental background and gave them for interpretation to pious theologians who knew nothing about oriental ideas and little about the languages which explained them. The theologians of the Middle Ages built up theories and interpretations which are very ingenious but which have so completely distorted the meaning of many passages that, when their true significance is pointed out to us, it causes great surprise.

Just one example: Once I heard a very good preacher deliver a sermon on the words of Jesus, who, according to John 20:19, suddenly stood before his disciples and said, "Peace be unto you." I shall not analyze the sermon in detail, but the preacher returned again and again to the idea that these words must have given a great deal of inspiration and comfort to Jesus' hearers. The fact is that when Jesus said "Peace be unto you," he meant by those words exactly what the modern Moslem means when he says *Salaam aleikum*. The words correspond exactly, and they are merely equivalent to "Good morning"! A closer study of cuneiform literature will play havoc with some of the later theological interpretations and will permit the Bible after many centuries to pass on to us precisely the message which its original writers intended to convey. In all fairness, if we respect a book, we ought to give it a chance to deliver its message.

Chapter 11

IT IS generally believed that philosophical speculation began more or less with the Greeks and that the
ancient peoples never troubled their minds with
the why and how of things. Why this should be, it is
difficult to understand, especially in view of the high
degree of civilization reached in both Mesopotamia and
Egypt. We might be nearer the truth if we supposed that
philosophical speculations were considered by people in
general as useless and inconsequential and therefore not
worthy of being preserved in writing. This would not be
so very astonishing, since even today many people think
philosophy an impractical and useless mental exercise.

The Babylonians, however, did not think philosophy
useless, and they recorded whatever theories they had in
their documents. If we do not know more about them, it
is because such studies could never be popular; also, they
are chiefly in the ancient Sumerian language, and in
more or less incomplete form. It will take another fifty
years at least before a comprehensive chapter on ancient
philosophy can be written. But a beginning could be
made now because something has already reached us.

First of all, let us begin with a problem which could not
trouble the ancient philosophers of Mesopotamia. I refer
to the problem of evil, which has kept Christian theologians so busy. If God is holy and omnipotent, how

can sin have entered the world? The answer the Christians give is: through the fault of mankind; and so come the stories of original sin, which purport to have a biblical foundation.

The Babylonians, like the Greeks and Romans, did not consider their gods holy. Their deities were big and powerful and wise, but they made mistakes; in fact, here applies that witty saying of a modern philosopher: If God made man in his own image, man has returned the favor and made his god in his own image. Such were the old Babylonian gods, making and acknowledging mistakes. The problem of evil could not be posed on such a background.

But the Babylonians devoted a good deal of time to the problem of man's position in the universe. They did not wait until modern science pointed out to them the many resemblances between the physical shape of man and that of animals. They *knew* that they were closely related, and they knew also that the only real difference was that man possessed intelligence. Their gods too were intelligent, but they had something else that man didn't have: they possessed eternal life. Thus man was somewhere in between the gods and the animals. Unlike the animals, he was intelligent and therefore nearer the gods. Unlike the gods, he was mortal and therefore nearer the animals. How could this anomalous situation have arisen? Was it the fault of the gods or was it the fault of man? This theory arose: In our own beings we have something of the gods. Just as in the Bible man received from God something divine in the breath that gave life to that first image of clay, so among the Babylonians something of the gods was used in the making of the first man in that he was created out of a mixture of divine blood and earthly clay. This is one of the explanations given.

But in ancient myths we do not find the same uniformity that we strive for in our present beliefs. Variant myths sprang up in different centers, and each individual was free to accept or believe whatsoever pleased his fancy. The ancient peoples were not at all intolerant and would never have understood that "outside of the church there is no salvation." One explanation was followed immediately by others. I shall summarize here a typical story which seems to have enjoyed great popularity and which was so widely circulated that a copy of it has been found as far away from Mesopotamia as Egypt.

One of the gods had taken it upon himself to be the benefactor of mankind. It was he who warned the Babylonian Noah that the deluge was coming and that he had better prepare a boat. This friendly god took a very special liking to Adapa, a fisherman on the Persian Gulf. They must have spent a long time together because Adapa had a chance to learn from his friend, the god, a good many secrets known only to the gods. Knowledge, in ancient belief, carried with it power. Learned men *ipso facto* became dangerous men who had to be respected. Adapa therefore grew in knowledge and power. One day he was fishing, when the south wind, which the Babylonians pictured as a huge bird, overturned his boat. Had he been only a man, he might have cursed the wind, and that would have ended the matter, but Adapa was more than that. He had superhuman wisdom and took revenge by breaking a wing of the south wind. One day passed, two days, a week, and still the south wind didn't blow. The matter was duly reported to the chief of the gods, who inquired and found out about the incident. He immediately decided to call Adapa up to heaven and make him explain things.

The friendly god was very much worried about what would happen when this mortal went up for his interview with the gods. They would immediately find out that he knew too much, and Anu, the chief of the gods, might decide that such a being had no place in creation and kill him off. The friendly god, Ea, therefore began to set the stage so as to give his friend a chance to survive the ordeal. He told him to dress in mourning garments, put ashes on his head, and go to the door of heaven. Two gods who were on guard would ask, "Why are you in mourning, and why do you put ashes on your head?" To this the man should answer, "I am sad because the two gods So-and-so have left the earth and are now stationed in heaven." Since the guards of heaven were exactly the ones he was supposed to be mourning, he would start by making friends who might later plead for him. But in spite of this precaution Ea was still anxious, and so he gave this very special advice to his friend: "If Anu gives you garments to wear, put them on, but if he gives you food to eat or water to drink, refuse it. They will be the food of death and the water of death."

Thus instructed, Adapa went up to heaven. His interview with the guards came out very satisfactorily, and they immediately took a great liking to this poor mortal who still mourned them. They accompanied him up to the seventh heaven into the presence of the great god.

As Ea had correctly surmised, it took no time at all for Anu to discover that this man knew too much. Anu perceived also who might have been the betrayer of the heavenly secrets and gave Ea a good scolding, but the problem still remained. What should he do with a man who by his knowledge was no longer fit to be a man? It may have been because of the intercession of the friendly gods, or perhaps Anu was in a kindly mood, but, at any rate, he decided that, since the job had already been nearly completed, he might as well finish it and give to this man the food of life and the water of life. This would automatically turn him into one of the lesser gods. He commanded one of the attendants to bring the food, and it was placed before Adapa, who, however, remembered the warning that his friend had given him and refused to eat. This greatly astonished and somewhat angered the god. "Why, Adapa, dost thou not eat of the food of life?" Adapa was stubborn. He had decided not to die by poison. After a while Anu gave up. "Adapa, you have refused to eat of the food of life. Go back to the earth and die." Adapa was allowed to descend to the earth and presumably led a happy life, but he became old and died as all men do.

This story puts the blame for the failure to obtain eternal life both on man and also on the god who had advised him wrongly. We have other stories in Babylonian literature with more or less the same motif. The great Gilgamesh legend ends this way: The hero Gilgamesh had seen his friend and companion die. He had a vision of the underworld where all souls go and decided that he would do his very best to escape a place like that. He started, therefore, on a search for the plant of life. He was told that such a plant did exist on a far-distant island near the spot where the Babylonian Noah had been placed by the gods to live forever. Obviously, to give Noah eternal life, the gods had put at his disposal the plant of life, which when eaten would give him sufficient strength to resist death. The journey of Gilgamesh was full of adventures, but he finally reached the island, talked to Noah, and incidentally heard from him the complete story of the deluge. He found the plant, but, while he was crossing the water in his boat, a serpent came up from the water, snatched the precious plant from him, and took it away.

If the story teaches anything, it is that man cannot steal food which is reserved for the gods alone. The serpent evidently was one of the gods who had been commanded to take away from man what did not belong to him.

In the Bible we have again absolutely the same motif. Through the intervention of a serpent, Adam and Eve became acquainted with one of the divine secrets and were able to obtain "knowledge of good and evil," which simply means intelligence. When Jehovah found out that part of his knowledge, that is, some of the divine prerogatives, had been stolen, he became angry and said, "Behold, the man is become as one of us [gods] to know good and evil: and now, lest he put forth his hand, and take also of the tree of life, and eat, and live forever: . . . ." In other words, man had become half a god by obtaining intelligence. Lest he gain immortality also, and become altogether a god, he was driven out of the garden, and a special guard was put in front of the gate so that he could never come in again. Jehovah acted just about the way Ea thought Anu would act. He was a little kinder, since he had no thought of destroying the wretched mortal right away. He was less generous because he did not wish, as had Anu, to make him a god altogether. In the case of Jehovah and man it was partly man's fault and partly God's fault that mankind did not acquire immortality. Adam and Eve should have passed immediately from tree to tree and completed the work, once they had started it. The first chance gone, the gods saw to it that there wouldn't be another.

Other texts might be quoted that would illustrate the same thing. They are, however, in poor condition and not satisfactory for the present purpose. But it is evident that the whole cycle of stories has a philosophical background. The question as to why men were superior to animals and yet were not gods was one of the first to be attacked by the philosophers of ancient Babylonia.

They also speculated on the origin of civilization. How did man become civilized? They did not start with the idea that man had fallen from a higher state. Incidentally, neither did the Bible. That is all theological erudition which the simple biblical story will never support. The Babylonians were observers. They saw many backward peoples around them, and they recognized their own superiority. Since their civilization was so very old, they had no recollection of a time when they had not possessed well-built cities and flourishing fields. In fact, though they themselves had gone through a pastoral or nomadic stage, they did not remember it. They also spoke with evident scorn of the people who had no

141

houses, did not cultivate grain, and did not even bury their dead. They meant by this that the nomads had to bury their dead anywhere and abandon the graves without performing the necessary rites upon them at stated intervals.

Just a few years ago we succeeded in piecing together from a large number of tablets the complete story of an ancient Sumerian myth. Jokingly, I used to call it the Darwinian theory of the Sumerians. The myth must have been rather widely circulated, for many copies of it have already come to light. In common with the biblical story, a woman plays the prominent role, just as Eve did. But the resemblance ends there. Poor Eve has been damned by all subsequent generations for her deed, while the Babylonians thought so much of their woman ancestress that they deified her.

Mankind, we learn from this myth, at the beginning was in a savage state. Men ate the grass of the field, drank the water of stagnant pools as did the animals, wore no clothing, and apparently walked on all fours. This very low condition moved the gods-to-be, and they gave this backward man two great gifts. They created a deity who corresponds roughly to the Roman Ceres and personifies the cultivated cereals, and another god who represents domesticated animals. With both agriculture and domestication of animals, the previous unfortunate condition of man changed immediately. He had plenty of food and could begin his upward march. It is interesting to note that we moderns also mark the first step upward from a savage to a civilized state by the introduction of agriculture and domesticated animals.

Other myths are plentiful. There is one, not yet complete and therefore difficult to understand, which seems to date the upward march from the time when writing was introduced. This is certainly logical, since with writing came the definite transmission of knowledge from generation to generation; but for it we should never have been able to reach the position we now hold, whatever stage of advancement that may represent. Some of the tablets list several steps in the attainment of civilization, and it would appear that each step was made when some kind god granted to mankind the use of some special instrument, usually agricultural. This is also reasonable, since the different inventions may be considered milestones in the march of progress. It is strange that, to the best of my knowledge, we have not yet found a myth that considers the acquisition of fire a definite step in our development. The Prometheus myth has not as yet appeared in Babylonian literature, though, of course, it may do so at some later date. If, however, such should not be the case, it would be because the Babylonians themselves could not think of a time when they did not have fire. Without the possession of cereals and domesticated animals, fire would have been of slight value.

While the problem of original sin did not trouble the ancient philosophers, the problem of suffering did. In common with the Hebrews, the Babylonians did not believe that pious men would be rewarded in future life by being granted a more exalted position or a happier condition than sinners. The Hebrew Sheol and the Babylonian Arallu were desolate places where all the dead, whether good or bad, had to go. If there were any justice in this world, the righteous man should be rewarded for his good deeds during his life. If a man were good, religious, and worshiped the gods properly, he should have some assurance that as a reward his own life would be peaceful and happy. But this did not always happen. Why did the gods permit such injustice?

And so the same problem that worried Hebrews of antiquity, and which is so thoroughly discussed in the book of Job, troubled the ancient Babylonians also. They, too, had their story of the suffering just, and they came no nearer to solving the problem than the Hebrews did. Of course, it must be said that among ancient peoples of the Near East responsibility for bad actions was not limited to the actual culprit. The whole nation might suffer for the sin of one, and the sins of the fathers might be visited upon the sons of the sons for countless generations. Do you remember the question that was asked of Jesus? "Who has sinned—he or his father or his mother—that he should be born blind?" But even in the light of this philosophy the problem was insolvable. The only possible conclusion seemed to be that there was no real justice in this world.

That is why this ancient pessimistic view has been abandoned, and a doctrine of future reward made to take its place. But this stage was never reached in ancient times, and the only kind of life after death that the Babylonians could visualize was a very unhappy one. The place where they were all destined to go was an immense cave under the surface of the ground. There they would have remained, all naked, but for the fact that nature took care of them, and the souls of the dead were

144

covered with feathers like birds. For food there was nothing, since nothing could grow without the beneficial aid of sunshine. All they could eat was the clay of the ground. More than anything else, the unhappy departed souls longed for the open spaces and the beautiful sun that they could see no longer. The prospect was far from alluring, and that is the reason why Gilgamesh made a last attempt to secure immortality. The most they could hope for was an indefinite prolongation of life on this earth. Even the existence of the Babylonian Noah, cooped up on his little island, away from everywhere, was a hundred times better than the life of the great throng which was crowded into the underground cave.

If we include in the general field of philosophy the ancient cosmogonies or views of the beginning of the universe, then our subject expands without measure. Creation stories are, and always will be, plentiful. The most common Babylonian story, as we have seen, was based on the idea that at the very beginning there was watery chaos, represented by Tiamat. Out of it came the gods, who fought Tiamat so that they might bring about a state of order. This order they achieved by doing what the Bible describes as "dividing the waters that are above the earth from the waters that are below the earth." The flat ground was made out of one half of the dead dragon, and this floated on the waters below; the other half of the dragon was bent over the solid platform, and it kept the waters above from inundating the ground below. The waters below were presumably bitter and worthless, while those above were sweet and came down in the form of rain, moistening the ground and collecting into lakes and rivers. How and why the waters above did not mix with the waters below, the Babylonians did not explain, and neither does the Bible. We thus have this general picture: a beautiful arable surface floating on water; a perfectly solid sky, like an inverted bowl, under which according to plan moved the stars, the sun, and the moon. The next step was that of creating plants and animals. This was done, and in the Babylonian story, also, man comes last as a sort of crown to the whole work of creation. In this the cosmogony of the Babylonians is parallel to that of the Hebrews, and no doubt the Hebrews borrowed it from them.

But we have other Babylonian stories not so dramatic. In one of them a great mass of water is again presupposed. But the gods are already in existence and planning wise deeds. One of the wisest of them decides to create the earth. Through his divine command there occurs some sort of cataclysm that raises the dry land out of the waters. The work of putting things in order continues, and special limits are assigned to the waters above and below the earth, to the seas, and to the rivers. All these different bodies of water must keep within the limits that have been allotted to them. After that, either through a war of gods or through a process of special creation—the tablet does not say—different beings begin to appear. The order resembles that of the biblical story, and again mankind is the crowning accomplishment.

Chapter 12

THERE is no question but that the Babylonians played a large part in laying the foundations of our sciences. From the beginning of the second millennium B.C. they catalogued and classified with meticulous care everything that came under their observation, and this body of information was passed on to be reorganized or revised by the generations following.

Great strides were made at an early period in the field of medicine. But here I expect the objection that what they practiced was not medicine but magic. I am beginning to lose patience with this word "magic," which is used to cover a multitude of sins and has therefore lost all clear meaning. It is high time that it be discarded and replaced by some other term really conveying a definite idea. Most of what passes under the name of magic is science in its infancy. Many savage people, when they need rain, build a great fire making lots of smoke. They hope that when this cloud of smoke ascends into heaven the rain clouds will see it, draw near, and bring the much-desired rain. Of course, you and I know that this does not work. But is it so surprising that early peoples should have had such ideas? In our own time, in trying to bring about rain or ward off a hailstorm, the people of our own Southwest have sometimes lent a credulous ear to the suggestions of itinerant fakirs. No truth is discovered without a series of futile attempts and failures, and the negative result itself, if properly looked for, is already a step nearer the truth. Suppose a chemist is trying to discover a formula. He sits down in his laboratory and spends his entire time experimenting. Every one of his attempts results in failure, and when he dies all he leaves is a complete record of his experiments. Shall we say that the life of that scientist has been wasted? Not at all. The next scholar who takes up the same problem will not need to repeat all the previous mistakes. He can go on and finally reach the goal. However, the accomplishment of the second would never have been possible but for the failures of the first. In other words, had we not had in the past that series of failures that we despise and throw away under the name of magic, our sciences would not exist. We should now be making the mistakes that the older scholars quite obligingly made in the past.

After this introduction let us look for a moment at Babylonian medicine. There were many physicians in those times, as we can see from the titles frequently following the names of important people. In fact, the art of medicine had become so important in the common life that it had to be regulated by law, and many sections of the Hammurabi Code are especially devoted to surgery. The surgeon is told exactly what he should charge for a minor operation and what for a major one. Prices differed for a rich gentleman, a poor laborer, and a slave. There is something to be said for this, but the Code goes a little too far. It specifies a fine for injury to unimportant people, and bodily punishment up to the loss of a hand

A PHYSICIAN'S CYLINDER SEAL LEFT THIS IMPRESSION. NOTE
THE SURGICAL (?) INSTRUMENT

of the physician for injury to a man of importance. We
can understand this, considering that higher fees brought
with them greater responsibility. But the Code goes even
farther; if the physician performs a major operation and
kills the son of a nobleman, then his own son will have to
be killed.

These provisions have sometimes been denounced as
harsh and unjust. Moreover, it has been emphasized
that it was a time when people had not yet discovered the
existence of microbes and the danger of infection, and so
the number of unsuccessful operations must have been
much higher than today. Consequently, it has been
urged that, if the provisions of the Code had really been
carried out to the letter, physicians would have lost not
only all their money in fines but also their hands, their
family, and their own lives. How indeed could surgeons
operate under such circumstances? The real explanation

149

is that the Code provided only for extreme cases in which the fatal result was undoubtedly due to carelessness or neglect on the part of the surgeon. None of the penalties would be imposed without a regular trial before a court. It must be remembered that there were no medical associations to uphold definite standards of medical practice, and some measures of control were necessary. Nor is it unreasonable to suppose that the provisions of the Code did force the ancient surgeons to exercise more care in the performance of their duties than might otherwise have been the case.

So much for surgery. Healing herbs and potions were also prescribed. Medical texts corresponding to the textbooks used and studied by modern physicians have come down to us by the hundreds. There is first a description of the symptoms, followed by the prescription, and then an incantation to the gods:

If a man has fever and a cold sweat covers his body and he has a pain in his stomach and he shivers, take the root of the plant so-and-so; put it in a mortar and grind it to a fine dust; take a pinch of the plant so-and-so; mix it with the dust; make a potion and give it to the patient to drink, before night. Then recite such and such an incantation.

Descriptions of diseases are often so clear that modern physicians can recognize them. In some cases, as might be expected, important symptoms have not been noticed, so that the patient in question might have suffered from any one of two or three different diseases.

As for the actual medical value of the herbs and drugs used, we are in doubt. Most of their names are still unknown to us, and, since they are never described, it will be some time before we can form a very definite idea concerning the effectiveness of the ancient pharmacopoeia. But there, again, the Babylonians were very observant people, and there is no question but that the remedies were based on a large body of experience. It is therefore easy to imagine that the drugs must have been more or less effective. Amusing though it may be, it is a fact that olive oil mixed with beer was the ancient predecessor of our oil shampoo and alcoholic massage as a "remedy" for baldness. And few are aware that our prescription of warm oil for earache was anticipated twenty-five hundred years ago by the Assyrians. Such remedies, and hundreds of others more important than these, seem to have served the ancients very well.

Some may object that this fact does not make ancient medicine a true science—that it was altogether empirical. But so was modern medicine up to a very few years ago, and so it remains even now in many of its fields. What we object to most is the incantation. Why should a prayer to a god be mixed up with purely scientific work? We prefer it otherwise. We first call the physician, get a prescription, and then summon the minister to pray for the sick. We want our science and our religion to be administered by different persons. In ancient times one and the same person attended to both.

Of course, in the field of medicine the Babylonians had some curious ideas. When they observed that a man who was sick got well after a time but that someone else in his family was stricken by the same disease, they explained it by saying that the demon of the disease had passed from one person into another. Up to a certain point we agree with them in this; but we do not call the cause of the sickness a demon; we call it a bacterium or germ. Just what their conception of this demon was, we do not know. There is certainly no reason for assuming that they imagined every demon to be some sort of little Mephistopheles with horns on its head and a barbed tail simply because a few of them are grotesquely represented. All that the medical texts tell us is that fever, for example, is caused by a demon that gets into the body and eats it away. They thought of this demon of fever as lurking at the crossways, ready to pounce upon the poor inoffensive pedestrian.

After having established the fact that some diseases were caused by demons and that these could pass from one to another, the ancient priest-physicians decided on another experiment. Why not give the demons some medium into which they could pass, thereby leaving in peace the other members of the household? So they decided to take a lamb or a kid, put it close to the patient, and try to effect the transference of the disease. After performing whatever rites they thought useful for the purpose, they took the animal, killed it, and looked inside the carcass to see whether the operation had been successful. If the animal presented a diseased liver or lung, and some symptoms of the patient's disease, they would infer that it had succeeded. Of course, we know now that it could not have succeeded. But let us remember that the operation did not do the patient any harm. It certainly helped a good many suffering people with the certitude that they were being cured. Most modern physicians know that if they succeed in persuading a patient that

A GROTESQUE ASSYRIAN DEMON

he is on the way to convalescence, half the battle is already won. In this sense, the ancient "magical" formula was truly comparable to the bedside technique of the modern physician.

The system was wrong, but the idea of demons has continued in vogue up to our days. It was the system which Jesus employed in curing the lunatics of Galilee, and it is the system which the Arabs today use to get rid of some of their afflictions. And, while the practice was all wrong, the idea is strangely in accordance with our own. We have reversed the process and improved upon it. We take an animal and pass into it the disease of a man. Then we take part of this animal and pass it into a diseased man to effect a cure, or into a well man to prevent the disease from attacking him. This time, in spite of many conscientious objectors to vaccinations and inoculations, we can say that the system works. But when we know that our modern practice is so very close to that of the ancients we have no right to discredit them by calling them "magicians."

By 2000 B.C., the Babylonians had already formulated the fundamental laws of mathematics—laws which were not rediscovered by the Greeks until fifteen hundred years later. So advanced were they that many an Assyriologist gets lost in trying to analyze a list of figures, the interrelations of which he will never be able to grasp unless his mathematical knowledge is greater than is generally the case. In mathematics the ancients worked under what at first sight appears to be a great handicap: their system of numerals. While from the earliest periods the decimal system, based on the primitive method of counting by the fingers, was already in use, from the same early times Babylonian scholars had evolved the sexagesimal system, in which the unit was not ten but sixty. For the complicated calculations which were the joy of the Babylonian mathematicians, the sexagesimal system may even have been superior to the decimal. For while the decimal system permits exact factoring only by 2, 5, and 10 (when other numbers are employed we have either a continuing decimal or a difficult fraction), sixty, the unit of the sexagesimal scheme, can be factored evenly by 2, 3, 4, 5, 6, 10, 12, and 15, and, further, by 9, 16, and other numbers if the process is carried to the next lower order. Thus the use of the sexagesimal system, which never disappears completely from Babylonian calculations, may not have been due, as one might think, to Babylonian conservatism, but rather to the greater adaptability and elasticity of the system. Actually, the whole system was so effective that it has imposed itself upon the world. Few people realize that we still follow it in some cases. We still divide the circle into 360 parts, the hour into 60 minutes, and the minute into 60 seconds.

There are other great contributions made by the mathematicians of those days that are generally ignored. The Babylonians were the first to give to figures a definite value according to their position in a number. When we write 5,300,375, the first figure, 5, is written exactly the same way as the last, but, while the last represents only units, the first represents millions. Many ancient peoples have had a special sign for the millions, another for the hundred thousands, and so on. The revelation that figures could alter the numerical value according to their position in a group has been assigned to a good many other peoples, while the Sumerians, who first discovered it, have been forgotten. Further, it has only recently been known that the Babylonians had a highly developed algebra, as well as geometry.

They early discovered, or came very near to discovering, a sign for zero. In a volume by a great mathematician there is this statement: "It needed all of the philosophical insight of the Hindus to take nothing and represent this nothing with a concrete symbol." I am sorry to disagree with a very great scholar, but the philosophical insight of the Sumerians was more than sufficient. When they wrote down a series of figures, if in one of the columns representing, let us say, the hundreds, no figure appeared, they would write in its place a sign that meant "not." They were afraid that later on someone recopying the tablet would not notice the empty space and would put the figures close together, therefore altering their value. That "not" corresponds approximately to our "naught," which in itself is the same as the zero. When it is said that they came "very near" to discovering it, it is because they did not use this "not" consistently. Just like us, they could get around the difficulty in a simpler way. They could say three bushels and fifteen pints, omitting completely the smaller subdivisions of the bushel, such as the peck. But the idea was there, and they wrote down their "not" at least two thousand years before the Hindus succeeded in inventing a symbol, if they ever did, for something that never existed. And about 500 B.C., the famous Nabu-rimanni—Naburianus to the Greeks—actually employed what was formerly a "ditto" sign as a true zero in his astronomical tables for the calculation of the new moon and eclipses.

No one can deny that the Babylonians were the fathers of astronomy. Kidinnu (367 B.C.), whose name was known to the Greeks though it is ignored by astronomers today, earned such a place in the development of the science as to make his name worthy of being set by the side of that of Kepler, Copernicus, or Galileo. In their work the old Babylonian astronomers were greatly aided by the climate. There is little rainfall in Iraq, and from April to October not a cloud mars the sky. Also, in those times the air was not polluted by the smoke of industrial establishments, so that even without the aid of telescopes observers could learn a good deal from the study of the clear oriental sky. They observed the movements of the planets and marked down the results of their observations. They noted every single phenomenon with such great care that they were able to notice even the changes caused by the precession of the equinoxes. Eclipses of the sun, moon, and stars were so carefully described that part of the ancient chronology has now been fixed without fear of mistake by just such occurrences. It is an extraordinary fact that modern astronomers have not yet been able to accumulate a series of astronomical observations as long as the Babylonian. For the longest known series of modern observations—that at Greenwich—was begun only in 1750. And the Babylonians had crude observations for many centuries before their official series began.

But here, again, I am certain that someone will interpose an objection. True, the ancient Babylonians worked in astronomy, but they were astrologers and observed the movements of the stars in order to foretell human events, and their whole standpoint was wrong. There is no doubt that astronomy was connected with astrology, just as chemistry developed from alchemy and the search for the philosopher's stone. In fact, no progress of any kind has ever been made which did not start either with a series of blunders or with an entirely wrong hypothesis. And yet I am not at all certain that the astronomers of those times looked upon the stars only because they wanted to read in them the events of their own future or the future of their country. That this was the motive which started the observations is readily granted. But even at an early time the practical problems of calendar-making and time adjustment demanded a study of the heavenly bodies. Further, just as the true scholar in modern times always works for his own pleasure and interest, quite oblivious as to who pays the bill or what the motive, so I am sure that many of the ancient scholars must have worked faithfully for science, utterly unmindful that the funds supporting the work came from the royal exchequer and were given chiefly because the king hoped to benefit thereby. It is the same old question of "pure" versus applied science. In any case, before we cast our stone, let us first purify our libraries and newspapers of the works and articles dealing with astrology. Three thousand years of development should have helped us more.

The geographic knowledge of primitive peoples was rather rudimentary. They started with wrong conceptions of the physical shape of the earth. They thought the earth was flat and the sky shaped like a dome. They had also some notion of a great ocean. This was supposed to be an immense sea surrounding the great island which represented the existing terra firma. The Pillars of Hercules even in Roman times marked the extreme limit that men could safely reach. School children know that this conception still existed in the days of Columbus, and the world-maps of medieval times seem to us curious and distorted charts.

The Babylonians held many of these ideas; in fact, they initiated some of them. They believed that on the earth, on a Mount of Gods, dwelt the chief deities. This conception was shared and passed on, though under different forms, among almost all the ancient peoples. In Greece, for instance, the abode of the gods was known as Mount Olympus, and in Moslem religion it still persists as the place where the faithful go after death. Again like other ancient peoples, the Babylonians thought that there was a huge cave under the earth which was the abode of the dead. This corresponds to the Hades of the Greeks and Romans and to the Sheol of the Hebrews. The Babylonians also believed that there was somewhere an island where a few minor deities resided, and as a special grant a mortal might be sent there to live forever as a semidivine being. But all these ideas were very hazy, and the places concerned were not indicated very definitely on the world-maps. For although the Babylonians were scientifically minded and have given us maps which aim to picture the world as they understood it, they themselves recognized that on this question they were on difficult ground; and so they preferred to devote their attention to maps of places they actually knew.

159

A DRAWING OF THE CITY NIPPUR ON AN ANCIENT TABLET

Such maps, scratched on clay tablets, indicate the courses of rivers and the positions of seas. One of the oldest of them, dating well into the third millennium, was discovered not very long ago. It does not, incidentally, cover a very large area of ground, and it must have

160

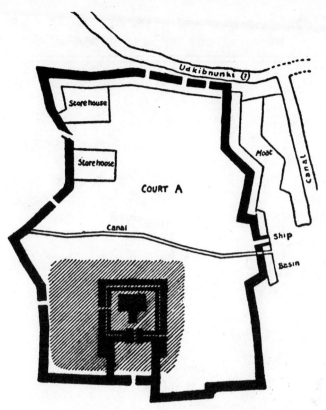

PLAN OF NIPPUR, AFTER EXCAVATION

been used to establish the exact boundaries of an estate.
Later maps have been found in different cities, and
among them is one especially worthy of notice, that of
the city of Nippur, which was found by excavators in one
of the earliest campaigns and was used by them as a guide
for conducting the excavations.

While we do not possess a great number of maps covering very large regions, we know through many sources

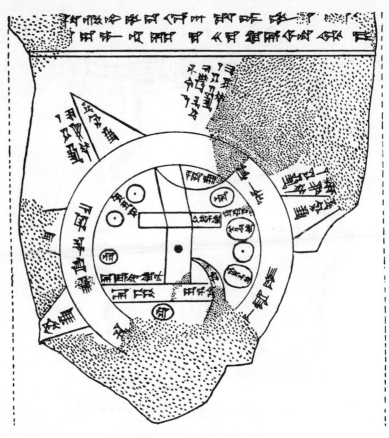

A BABYLONIAN WORLD-MAP

that the Babylonians were well acquainted with the people surrounding them and had not only a good knowledge of, but a great interest in, the highways connecting their land with adjacent countries. Their traveling salesmen went everywhere, and we find Babylonian kings protesting to Egyptian pharaohs that the highways through

162

Syria and Palestine are unsafe and that their commercial employees are being robbed by the natives. The Babylonians had also traveled extensively through the north and must have reached the Black and Caspian seas. We know little concerning the real extent of their eastern travels because as yet practically no archeological work has been done in that area.

However, scattered bits of information make us conscious that contact with very distant regions was always maintained. That the ancient travelers must have gone far away from their native land is proved by the materials they used, especially their jewels. Some of the materials they employed—tin, for instance—are not found within their land. Some scholars even thought at one time that the Sumerians procured their tin from England! Spices

AN ANCIENT "BLUEPRINT"

must certainly have come from Arabia. How far the geographic knowledge of the ancients went is indicated by the fact that sometimes in texts describing the military exploits of their kings we find long lists of foreign names which are so well known from countless other documents that we can locate them exactly on the map. And so, in our archeological labors, we shall have to go far beyond the limits of Iraq and Mesopotamia in order to trace the extensive wanderings of the ancient travelers.

Chapter 13

THE difficult art of writing on clay necessitated a long period of schooling. I should think that it took the Assyrian scribes as long to master their writing as it takes the pupils of today to acquire a good knowledge of reading and writing English. Just as today, the pupils could decide whether to enter a regular school or to work under a private teacher, but it is likely that most of the would-be scribes followed the latter system. The regular schools were attached to the temples and were therefore at some distance from one another. Scribes, however, who could be depended upon to teach were scattered everywhere, even in the small towns. Just as in the Middle Ages an expert craftsman would take under his protection some young boy as an apprentice to whom he taught his trade, so most of the scribes had some youth who was ambitious to enter the profession. However, the relationship between this teacher and his apprentice was even closer than it was in later centuries. The scribe "adopted" his apprentice as his own son, and the relationship lasted until the young man was able to enter the profession as a regular member. I was puzzled, while studying a certain group of documents, by the excessive number of persons who called themselves sons of Mr. So-and-so, the scribe. The explanation finally came to me that these young men were not really sons of the scribe but his pupils, who had been left by their parents under his special guidance. We have here a picture which is not rare in antiquity, of the master going about, practicing his profession, followed by his group of apprentices who are trying to learn from the example of their teacher. Such private tutoring would be quite sufficient to prepare scribes for the usual commercial branches of the craft. They could learn by heart the different formulas for all the needed documents, and they could be relied upon to take dictation in the case of private correspondence.

For more extensive training they had to go to the regular schools. We might say that private tutoring would correspond to the high-school course and enable its graduates to enter a business life. But only the schools that were located always in the vicinity of the great temples had facilities for the study of the sciences and literature. There one could begin with the very rudiments of writing and continue until one was ready to become a priest or a scientist in the ancient meaning of the term.

We have recovered from the ruins of the cities "textbooks" used by the pupils in their endeavor to master the language. Such "textbooks" differ from ours, of course, in the fact that they were really tablets of clay and so were too unwieldy to move from one place to another. But while the ancient manual for learning how to write may not have been so comprehensive and compact as one that our children can buy for a few cents, the principle adopted was exactly the same. I remember that, when I went to primary school, we used to have penmanship books in which each alternate line contained a calli-

AS IN OUR ONE-ROOM COUNTRY SCHOOL ARE THE BENCHES IN THIS
EARLY SCHOOLROOM

graphic model, perfectly written in longhand, which we
were expected to reproduce as closely as possible in the
blank line immediately below. We still have the calligraphic models of the ancient schools, and the only difference from ours is that, instead of having the teacher's
models on alternate lines, they have them on the left-
hand side of the tablet, leaving the right-hand side for
the pupil. We can picture the young student after his
painful effort to reproduce his text, bringing his work for
the teacher to examine, and we can easily imagine that
many signs were immediately pointed out as being in-

correct: this sign had one wedge too many, another lacked an absolutely essential wedge; sometimes the signs were out of alignment, or were so crowded that it was impossible to distinguish one from another, while others were incorrectly spaced so that words were broken at the wrong places. We can notice all these mistakes today, and we can correct the exercises just as did the ancient teacher.

Once the copy was completed and duly commented upon, it was unnecessary for the teacher to start all over again and write down the calligraphic model for the next pupil. All he had to do was to pass his stylus over the first pupil's work and so flatten it out that the signs would disappear. Then the tablet was ready to be inscribed again. Of course, after having been used a number of times, either the clay became so dry as to be unsuitable for writing, or the tablet was so flattened out that it could no longer be used. Sometimes such tablets were thrown into the wastebasket, from which archeologists have rescued them with great care a long time after. Or perhaps the teacher decided to cut off altogether the right-hand side, which was the pupil's side, and leave his own model to be used again for copy purposes by students who did not need to have the model placed so closely before their eyes. Thus we have a large number of mutilated tablets, of which only one half of each has reached us. The pupil this time would place that beautifully written half-tablet in front of him, take a piece of clay, make it into a tablet, and try to reproduce his model to the best of his ability.

Of course, we can always read the pupil's writing when

we have at hand the teacher's model. It isn't equally easy when the model has not been preserved with it. We have found some of these independent efforts on the part of students so very badly written as to make it impossible for a decipherer to recognize more than a few signs. Obviously the teacher had made a mistake and trusted too much in the ability of his pupil in letting him go his own way when he still needed long practice with easier exercises.

These school exercises, written and erased and rewritten, are the earliest form of a palimpsest. There is one special type of school exercise which is the palimpsest par excellence. This time the pupil did not go to the trouble of preparing a tablet in the usual rectangular shape. He took a lump of clay, rolled it in his hands in the shape of a ball, flattened one side of it against a plane surface, and wrote on the flat portion. His work done, he rolled the tablet into a ball once more, flattened it again, and he had his writing material ready for the next exercise. The process could go on all day, and the writing material would always be perfectly good. We have found large numbers of these "lens-shaped" tablets; in the beginning they were a source of serious trouble to archeologists, who did not know what to make of them, especially as their contents were most varied.

When the teacher decided to give the students some work, he had before him in the temple school as many types of texts as he wished to choose from. For easy exercises he might pick up a list of signs and have the pupils practice writing them. This would correspond to our learning the letters of the alphabet, the only difference

AN EARLY "COPY-BOOK" WITH TEACHER'S MODEL INSCRIPTION

being that the group of signs is infinitely more varied and takes much more time to master. The next step would be to take a list of these same signs accompanied by their different phonetic values or ideographic meanings. Still another step might be to copy down portions of dictionaries containing complete lists of all the stones, animals, cities, or gods. After all this more or less elementary work had been mastered, the pupils were ready for literary texts. A portion of an epic or a psalm would be given them to reproduce as closely as they could.

It goes without saying that the material from the temple schools is very important, since it is nearly always taken from the classics and the manuals kept in the large libraries. The trouble for the Assyriologist is that such school texts represent "pages" copied at random, and stories appear without beginning or end. The pupil generally stopped either when he got tired or when school hours were over. Many such fragments of stories have been misinterpreted by scholars who did not realize that they were just "pages" from a book and not stories complete in themselves. However, since more or less the same text was copied by all the students, we often find the same story overlapping on many school tablets. One student may have begun just where another stopped, and the next one may have written down the second half of the first production and the first half of the second. Another thing happened which is also easy to explain. Ambitious pupils generally started copying a book from the beginning. Of course, they grew tired before they had gone very far, but it generally happens that the first "chapter" of all important works has come to us through countless copies made by these pupils. As the work proceeded, the copies thinned out until at the end we are left only with whatever fragments we can get of the original textbook.

Judging from the differing signs used in the same exercises by various pupils, students must also have taken dictation. Since there were many possibilities of putting down the same sound with different signs, we find in the texts considerable disagreement as to the signs employed, which, however, is very useful to us inasmuch as it proves that all the signs employed for any one sound had approximately the same phonetic value.

Besides taking dictation, all students had a certain amount of arithmetic; and the four operations—addition, subtraction, multiplication, and division—doubtless gave as much trouble to the students of old as they do to our children. All this work was preparatory, and it was followed by instruction in the higher branches qualifying for the different professions.

As a source for our knowledge of the important textbooks used in those times, we have accordingly, first, the original temple library containing all the classics and, then, the faulty copies of these texts made by the pupils in the school. To these were later added the royal libraries. In Babylonia, as in other ancient countries, political power was closely associated with religion. Even in our twentieth century we have not yet completely shaken off "the divine right of kings." And yet long ago in Babylonian times political power gradually began to rid itself of church control. It was necessary then, as today, to fight in order to keep the government free from religious influences. Even when the kings had asserted themselves and were powerful enough to retain their hold on the land without the help of the church, they generally tried to keep on good terms with the religious group by making large grants to the temples, freeing them from taxation, and helping them to the best of their ability. I may be accused of cynicism, but I believe that the church retained his good will by seeing to it that a pious king got good omens from the gods for anything he was planning to do. The fight was undercover, but it was there

ASSYRIAN SECRETARIES TAKING DICTATION

nonetheless; and, with the increase of royal prestige, it was thought wise by some of the more intelligent kings to restrict the influence of the church in education. If the church had libraries, then the kings also could have them. We thus find some of the later Assyrian kings, the very same personages who are generally depicted as ruthless destroyers, taking the lead in encouraging and reviving art and science. We see them also sending their own scribes throughout the land for the purpose of collecting all the important works gathered in the temples.

We still have a letter of a king who does not name himself but who is probably the famous Ashurbanipal. The contents are so interesting that I shall quote some passages verbatim:

Word of the king to Shadunu: It is well with me; mayest thou be happy. When thou receivest this letter, take with thee these three men [names given] and the learned men of the city of Borsippa, and seek out all the tablets, all those that are in their houses, and all those that are deposited in the temple of Ezida.

The king continues with a list of the important works which he especially wants and then concludes:

Hunt for the valuable tablets which are in your archives and which do not exist in Assyria and send them to me. I have written to the officials and overseers . . . . and no one shall withhold a tablet from thee, and when thou seest any tablet or ritual about which I have not written to thee, but which thou perceivest may be profitable for my palace, seek it out, pick it up, and send it to me.

There is no doubt that the scribes carried out the royal commands with all diligence because we have actually recovered, in the ruins of Nineveh, a great number of texts from the library of this ancient monarch. But the work that these later Assyrian kings did was more than that of merely collecting and recopying the material found in ancient libraries. After they had copied texts written in the Sumerian language, the task the kings set themselves was to retranslate this whole mass of material into the vernacular and adapt it to the needs of the time. The old Sumerian stories were published as they were found, with an interlinear translation in the Assyrian language. It must have required an immense amount of time and a great number of learned scholars to bring this work to completion. The royal courts at this time must have been centers of culture as notable as those of the patrons of science during the Renaissance. Notwithstanding their great array of learning, the translators must have had their troubles in interpreting the old texts, for the language had been dead more than a thousand years. It is an achievement of modern science that we can now correct some of the translations made in those days.

At present the only royal library with which we are at all well acquainted is that of Ashurbanipal, which fortunately was found at the very beginning of Mesopotamian excavations. Scholars put in possession of such a large number of bilingual texts could immediately tackle the decipherment of Sumerian. But while Ashurbanipal's library—and that not in its entirety—is the only one which has reached us, we have grounds, as we have said before, for believing that other and greater kings, such as Sargon of Assyria, had preceded him in this type of scientific undertaking. Excavations made a long time ago in other royal palaces also revealed a large number of tablets, but in those times the importance of these inscribed "bricks," as the finders called them, had not been recognized. It appears that they were thrown back into the dump, where they still are, awaiting renewed and more up-to-date archeological work to rescue them from oblivion. It would thus seem that libraries are no modern discovery.

Whether the Assyrian libraries were open to the public or not is hard to say. They may have been; their lawbooks certainly had to be kept available for lawyers. Of course, only a negligible percentage of the lay population would have been able to use the various books stored on their shelves. Still, I hope that we shall find definite proof some day that even public libraries are not such an innovation as most people think.

Chapter 14

A FTER all this, no one will be surprised to learn
that slowly, by piecing together materials found
in different parts of the country, we are able to
reconstruct the daily habits of the ancient peoples so that
they themselves come to life. However, it is not with this
slow process of reconstruction that this chapter will deal.
I am referring here to the swift emergence into full light
of a people whose very name was practically unknown.
These people appear suddenly out of complete darkness
and their appearance is accompanied by such wealth of
detail and clarity of presentation that, in spite of the fact
that they are newcomers on the scene of history, we can
learn more about some phases of their daily life than we
know about the corresponding aspects of the daily life
in Greece and Rome.

A few years ago, while I was in Iraq, Miss Gertrude
Bell, late director of antiquities for Iraq, spoke to me
about a special kind of tablet which had been coming into
the local markets and had puzzled scholars because of the
contents. Owing to the archeological interest of a physician, the provenience of the tablets had been discovered,
and Miss Bell invited me to start excavations in the hope
that we might recover more documents of the same kind.
Excavations were begun, though not in the exact spot
designated, and immediately a magnificent villa, obvi-

ously the residence of some ancient magnate, was brought to light. During the very last days of excavation we suddenly came upon a little room containing the ancient archives. Over a thousand tablets were found lying there in extreme confusion, though evidence pointed to the fact that they had originally been placed in rectangular baskets and kept in perfect order. When the house collapsed, a large number of the tablets had escaped damage, and for three or four days we were busily occupied in extracting and packing them for transportation. We made a study of them after they reached America and were soon convinced that we had the complete archives, through four or five generations, of one family in the ancient city of Nuzi. For the next four years excavations were continued in the same locality and about three thousand more tablets, belonging to other families or to temple archives, were recovered.

This group of documents presented one peculiar characteristic. They were written in Assyrian, but obviously the people among whom they originated were imperfectly acquainted with the language and so had violated the accepted rules of spelling and grammar. Moreover, foreign words were frequently interspersed with the Assyrian, and practically all the people mentioned bore foreign names. Furthermore, the contracts were based on laws and customs quite divergent from the laws and customs of the rest of the land. Thus we have a picture of a life that was neither Babylonian nor Assyrian. For no family of antiquity have archeologists ever found documents one-fourth as numerous or extending over so long a period of time. Closer study, and the fact that one of the tablets was a letter from a king whom we knew, placed the whole group somewhere around the fifteenth and fourteenth centuries B.C. The records referred chiefly to trade and real estate transactions; through them we could follow the rise and fall of the great Tehiptilla family.

One could write at great length on this "House of Tehiptilla." To begin with, the founder inherited a good-sized collection of houses, fields, and orchards, situated partly in the city and partly in the scattered towns and villages near by. Then he proceeded aggressively to enlarge his patrimony. With our insufficient knowledge of the prevailing ethical and moral standards of the time, it would be hasty to pass judgment on the actions of this ancient "capitalist." At all events, it can be said that his methods were strictly legal according to the letter of the law, even if legal means were employed to circumvent existing ordinances—a beautiful indication of the "modernism" of Tehiptilla!

Tehiptilla's sons and grandsons did the best they could, but slowly the power and prestige of the family began to decline. Invasion by an enemy, probably the Assyrians, appears to have been the final disaster, and the family practically disappears from the scene. The attack must have been a serious one, for we have contemporary records of the losses suffered not only by the family under discussion but also by other rich landlords of the city. The horses, cattle, and sheep which they lost in the raid are carefully enumerated, and the loss of independence can easily be surmised from the fact that Assyrian names of the months begin to supplant the local ones.

Nevertheless, the inhabitants of Nuzi were not entirely

THE
AUTHOR
AT NUZI

UNCOVERING THE PAST AT NUZI

subjugated, for there is evidence of a second raid. This time the invaders must have succeeded, for all the houses were found burned to the ground, and here and there within their precincts were bodies of the unburied dead. We are not certain who the perpetrators of this last outrage were because no document remains to tell us the story, but we do know that the destruction of Nuzi followed a period of unrest in which the peoples of the region were fighting for supremacy. At any rate, whoever brought about the overthrow of the city did such effective work that its ruins remained untouched for many hundreds of years.

It is very interesting—and pathetic—to follow through these documents the methods employed by Tehiptilla

180

and other rich landlords in gaining control of the land owned by the poor peasants. Evidently a local law forbade the peasants to sell their land. This was probably not due to any philanthropic motive but to the fact that the peasants had to have something to live on and land to cultivate if they were to pay taxes. The landlords did not violate the law but evaded it in a very ingenious way. Since time immemorial it had been customary for the people of Babylonia and Assyria to adopt persons who would take care of them in their old age. Suppose a childless couple found the work on their fields too heavy. They would adopt a young man and stipulate that they would give him all their possessions provided he would give them as long as they lived a certain amount of grain, a relatively small amount of oil, and the necessary clothes. How much they were to receive always varied with the value of the goods they could offer. If the adopted son kept his part of the contract, the inheritance went to him. This was really an early form of what today is called an annuity, whereby in return for a consideration an insurance company will guarantee an individual an amount of money proportionate to the premium he pays. The rich landlords of Nuzi immediately seized upon this custom and began to make the poor peasants adopt them as sons, so that they could either share in the inheritance of the real children or get all of it. If they did not promise to give a regular annuity, a lump sum which was called a gift would do just as well.

This system was used extensively, so that we find the very same man as the adopted son of three or four hundred peasants. That he was not a lone son we can also

NATIVES TRAMPING OUT OLIVE OIL

learn from the court proceedings, which are among the documents recovered. The fathers accused their son of wanting more than had been stipulated or of not having kept his part of the agreement. The documents generally keep up the fiction of "sonship," but sometimes the scribes forget and use words that clearly betray what the relationship really was. The practice must have proved very convenient, for sometimes we find on a single document a wholesale adoption. Five or six peasants adopt the same man and bequeath to him their property. Each receives as a "gift" an amount of money, grain, or the like, equal to a portion of the value of the property "willed," and remains on his former land cultivating it for his "child." The poor wretches, of course, gave up all claim to ownership. Consequently, there developed throughout the land a system of peonage with results even worse than those which the law had set out to avert. For the adoption could never be voided; this explains its great popularity with the landlords.

In many cases, however, the peasants refused to submit to this practice, and, when they were badly in need of money, they borrowed on the security of their fields. We have here a sort of mortgage, with the difference that the field which had been given as security immediately passed into the hands of the lender. At the end of a stipulated period of years, generally from five to thirty, a peasant had the right to redeem his field by giving back exactly the same sum of money which he had borrowed. No interest was charged because all through the period during which the field had been pledged the lender had cultivated it and appropriated all its produce.

When the mortgage fell due, the peasants, who had been having great difficulty in supporting themselves, could seldom pay back the sum of money they had borrowed. They were confronted by the dilemma: Should they let the time limit expire and lose the field altogether,

LEAVES FROM THE DIARY OF AN ANCIENT DAIRYMAN

PEASANTS HARVESTING GRAIN

or should they pledge it again for whatever extra money they might still be able to get? If the sum borrowed represented only a fraction of the value of the field, then some other rich man might be willing to pay off the first indebtedness and give a little more to the original owner so as to get possession of the field. Such being the case, quite often the first lender would himself grant a second loan on the same security and thereby be perfectly certain that the field would remain in his hands. Since all these transactions were fully written down and attested by witnesses, we may see in this practice a sort of approximation to the modern practice of the selling of commercial paper. Perhaps even closer is the analogy of the resale of a pawnshop ticket.

184

When neither adoption nor lending on collateral was advisable, from the landlord's point of view, a third way of getting around the law was that of exchanging property. It was not forbidden to exchange, but, while the letter of the law again was kept, the exchange as practiced was nothing less than a sale. A large and well-cultivated field would be exchanged for another that was either small or in such a condition as not to be tillable. Considering the disproportion in value, the landlord would make up the difference in cash. A good house might be exchanged for a hovel, and the difference in cash would amount to practically the full sale value of the property.

When the crops failed, as they frequently do in a country which has a very scanty rainfall, the peasants could avoid starvation only by surrendering their property. If they had none, then they mortgaged either themselves or their children into servitude with a document of exactly

A MODERN MILLER IN THE OLD LAND OF ASSYRIA

the same type as that which applies to houses or fields, or they sold their daughters to the landowners to be married by them to whomsoever they wished. These so-called marriage documents are crudely explicit: "The purchaser may take the woman for himself, may give her to one of his sons, or to one of his slaves. If the first husband dies, she may be given to a second, a third, a fourth, or a fifth, but from the house of the landlord she shall never go out." Some peasants, at the risk of getting less for their daughter, would stipulate that she could not be given as wife to a slave, for the wife of a slave became herself a slave, and her children would also be slaves.

It should not be deduced from this that the condition of women was low and degraded. Women had as many rights as men. They had all the civil rights of men, and even slave women had not completely lost their civil rights, for they appear in court and possess their own seal "signatures." Especially had the ladies of the wealthy class no reason for envying their husbands. They transacted all sorts of business, and we find the wife of Tehiptilla continuing the family traditions and being adopted as a daughter by a large number of peasants. In fact, she appears to have gone in for wholesale adoption, and with the same stroke of the hand, or perhaps of the stylus, she acquired as many as ten or fifteen new adopted fathers. While peasant women were given into marriage practically for breeding purposes, ladies took care to specify their own rights under the marriage contract: "If the woman So-and-so has children, the husband will not have the right to take a second wife. But if the woman has no children, then she will give her own handmaid to

186

the husband and she will have children through her. The children of the slave are to be reared by the husband as the children of the legal wife." We have here a close parallel to the story of Abraham, and we find that he had no right under this law to drive out Hagar and Ishmael.

The knowledge that possession of the family gods entitled one to a son's share in the father's inheritance is likewise derived from the Nuzi records and brings us close to the biblical story of Rachel and Jacob, mentioned in chapter 9. And in this connection there are among these records a number of real wills and testaments, in most of which we find the husbands leaving all their goods to their wives. These in their turn will distribute the goods among the children, who, while under maternal authority, have to obey their mother or run the risk of being disinherited.

Among the many family documents we have also a large number of court records giving a complete résumé of the law suits which have resulted favorably for the landlords. These are most interesting because the judges ask the witnesses questions and the witnesses answer in their own words. Then the decision is rendered. The loser must either pay a sum of money or become the slave of the winner until such time as he does pay. It was a very dangerous proceeding for peasants to bring their grievances to court because their chance of obtaining justice was slight, and most of them ended by losing their freedom. I have gone over these contracts with great care, trying to find out whether the judges made any effort to apply the law and be wholly impartial. Unfortunately, it is evident that they did not. The wealthy landlords kept their records in good order for generations, and quite

WATER FROM THE SPRING—FREE FOR ALL

often they could produce a document duly signed by many witnesses which attested their right to ownership and thereby closed the case. But the trouble was that the landlords had scribes of their own and a certain group of people who always acted as their witnesses. There was nothing easier, in view of the fact that the peasants did not know how to read, than to juggle a few figures or to alter measurements; the mistake would not be discovered for many years.

Yet in many cases a landlord, in spite of his well-kept archives, did not have documents to show; it is evident that those he had would not have proved his case. He then asked the peasant to produce his witnesses—impossible in most cases, since the transaction was so old as to go back two generations. Even if witnesses were produced, there was always a way to settle the case to the satisfaction of the landlord. The witnesses of both parties, having given under oath a contradictory version, were asked to have the gods prove the truth or falsity of their testimony. It was some sort of ordeal, probably the water test, which must have resembled those medieval ordeals in which the one who drowns has spoken the truth, and the one who saves himself has been rejected by the gods and is therefore to be put to death. The witnesses would suffer in either case. Those in charge of administering the ordeal must have shown some sort of partiality because it is always the plaintiff and his witnesses that refuse the ordeal; and so we read: "Because So-and-so and his witnesses fear to ask the gods, they lose their case and are condemned to pay," and so on.

This lack of justice in the law can be understood only

TURKOMAN WOMAN PREPARING A FEAST

by the fact that the judges were themselves members of the wealthy class and that vacancies in their ranks were filled by persons from their own group, The local king, who himself had little authority, probably did have the right to veto the appointment of a new judge, although he would very rarely be powerful enough to exercise the privilege.

Among these court records we find an interesting illustration of the way in which proceedings were recorded by the scribes. A case that might have consumed an hour had to be condensed into a tablet that could be read in one-tenth that time. Consequently, we have there no stenographic report but merely a summary. One day a scribe took a lump of clay and began to record one of these court proceedings. Before he had finished he realized that his tablet was too small and he could never write all the pertinent testimony upon it. He abandoned that tablet, made a bigger one, and started all over again. In spite of the fact that the second version must have been influenced considerably by the one that had been written immediately before, there is a wide divergence between the two. Speeches in direct quotation are reported quite differently, and, but for the fact that numerals, personal names, and the subject under discussion are absolutely the same, one would think that they were two different transactions. All praise to the modern stenographer who at least can pretend to have taken down the actual words!

Besides family documents we have those relating to the temple and the administration. The gods worshiped and the different cities from which offerings were received give us a very good idea of the geographical limits of the

190

district. We have there the city in arms, since all citizens, beggars, scribes, carpenters, or what not, had to possess their bows and arrows to use in case of war. The richer people had to keep in readiness a specified number of chariots, horses, and plate armor of different types adapted for men, horses, and chariots. These implements appear to have been inspected periodically, and their condition carefully noted. Some chariots, inspection showed, had loose boards, bows had no strings, horses were sick or useless. We have also what appears to be a distribution of booty of war between the important families, and among the booty we find slaves from different lands. But it is impossible even to try to summarize within the limits of a chapter what is contained in thousands of documents. The life of Tehiptilla and the character of the civilization of the city where he lived well deserve a complete book for themselves.

Chapter 15

IN A work which is based primarily on the information we derive from Babylonian tablets, one would not expect a chapter on art. True, some scattered information about arts and crafts can always be gathered from a study of the literature, but the unillustrated ancient texts could never be so satisfactory as our comprehensive art books, and such data as they give would not be sufficient for even a sketchy study. So I shall not attempt to gather what we do know from the literary productions.

Nevertheless, in spite of the inadequacy of the texts, clay tablets give us so much information about the whole field of art that we could never hope to obtain a better source anywhere else. We pointed out previously the interesting fact that people of the land, though unable to write, were able to sign documents because they carried their signatures around their necks. The very earliest seals, as these signatures are called, were probably nothing but amulets used to ward off evil influences; they were flat and made an impression either round or square or more or less oval in appearance. The representations on them were very crude, and it takes a good deal of imagination even to recognize human or animal forms. But this was long before clay had been introduced as a writing medium, and perhaps even before the invention of writing.

Gradually, however, as writing on clay tablets came to be more and more common, seals were better made and began to be used for signatures. It was then found that a little cylinder would be more convenient than a flat or stamp seal because it could be rolled across the wet clay of the document and would give a continuous impression. The cylinder seal had great vogue not only in Assyria and Babylonia, but also beyond these geographical limits. It was made of hard stone, sometimes even a precious stone

AN EARLY "STAMP" SEAL

if the owner could afford to procure such rare material. When economy had to be considered, then either soft stone or a portion of a conch shell was used. The artists of those times spent a great amount of ingenuity in engraving such cylinders, and we have in some of them diminutive works of art depicting scenes of all sorts. Poor people, who could not afford to hire a real artist, did the best they could, so that it is very difficult for us to distinguish a "primitive" seal from a later one. Sometimes what is primitive is the artist and not the period.

Today these small cylinders of stone are found through-

A NECKLACE OF BEADS ALL THE MORE PRIZED FOR ITS STAMP
SEALS

out the land. The modern Arab woman, with the help
of her admirers, sometimes collects a necklace made of
cylinders of different sizes and materials. It is easy to
string them together because each has a longitudinal
hole through which was passed, in ancient times, either
a string or some special device for hanging it around the
neck. Many modern archeologists have looked with envy
at such collections of ancient seals with which the proud
owner did not wish to part.

And yet, while the cylinders themselves are a very good
source of information, the very fact that they are general-

ly well preserved and of good appearance indirectly diminishes their value for an archeologist. Many of them have been found in different parts of the land since time immemorial and have been carried by their owners far away from their place of origin. Moreover, since they keep very well, it frequently happens that a peasant of modern times will find in his field a cylinder that dates back earlier than 2000 B.C. and add it to a collection of jewelry which has been made today. We thus have both the period and the provenience of these tiny works of art so completely mixed that it is quite difficult to base any kind of study on ancient seals and still remain on safe ground.

Another complication has arisen in recent times. Just as with scarabs in modern Egypt, so in Mesopotamia these cylinders have proved to be a good field for the forger of antiquities. It is relatively simple for a man who knows anything at all about engraving to duplicate such seals. Almost any kind of stone will do for material, and any kind of workmanship will pass. Unless the modern forger attempts to copy writing which he doesn't understand, and unless he draws entirely from his own imagination in making up the motifs, it is often absolutely impossible to distinguish a modern forgery from a genuinely ancient seal. A little forgery story was once told me by a dealer in antiquities in Baghdad, and I am certain that the story is true, especially because he himself gains nothing by telling it.

A few years ago there lived in Baghdad a certain Riza, undoubtedly a real artist, but one who had turned his talent to the manufacture of antiquities and had specialized in reproducing the little engraved cylinders. This was generally known, but the law could not touch him because he never attempted to sell his handiwork himself. One day a peasant went to my friend the dealer with a seal cylinder of unusual beauty; but he knew what he had, and consequently asked a rather high price for it. The dealer wanted the seal but at the same time did not like to pay the price asked. The usual oriental bargaining having failed, he told the peasant to leave the object and return in two days. By that time he would have studied the seal and would know if he could pay such a high price.

As soon as the peasant left, the dealer rushed to Riza and asked him to make a perfect duplicate of the seal. His intention was to refuse to buy in the end and to return to the owner the copy instead of the original. Riza lived up to his reputation. He produced such a good duplicate of the seal that it was difficult to distinguish one from the other.

Since his plan had succeeded so well, the dealer was now very happy. When the peasant appeared, he was shown both seals and was told that, considering the fact that another one, just as good as his own, was already on the market, the price asked for it was ridiculous, and he could take back his seal. But here something unexpected happened. The peasant did not want to miss a sale. He came down so much on the price that the seal had to be bought.

Some time later a good scholar, representing an important museum in Europe, came to look over the dealer's stock. He was a personal friend as well as a good cus-

tomer. Here was a chance to play a joke on him. The dealer showed him the counterfeit seal and asked for an opinion on it. The scholar was very enthusiastic. He mentioned a price that was tentatively accepted and asked permission to take the seal to his hotel for closer study. He would return it the next day.

Permission was duly granted, but the next day the scholar did not return. He had been detained by other business and, carrying the seal with him, had finally left the country. In due time came a check in payment for it from the museum. This was carrying the joke too far, since the dealer had never intended to cheat his good customer. He accepted the check but wrote back to his friend that in the meantime he had found out that the seal sold was a modern copy of an ancient original. Would he

197

please accept the original and return the copy? The museum authorities did not see it that way. They insisted that they had bought the right one and that the one sent later was a copy. They kept the first!

But, good or not, even if these seals were the very best source of information in the world, we could not use them in a study like ours, since we have limited ourselves to the information we can acquire from the clay tablet itself. However, the seals were made to be impressed on tablets, and in so far as they served that purpose they come within the limits we have set up. After a document had been completely written, the scribe affixed his own seal, equivalent to his signature, and then called on the witnesses in the order of their importance to do the same. Close to the impression of each seal, which appeared in relief on the wet clay, the scribe proceeded to write the name of the person to whom the seal belonged. For the first two or three impressions the best part of the unwritten section of the tablet was used. Less important witnesses had to place their "signatures" around the edges or in any other empty space they could find. Obviously some of the impressions are clear, while others are somewhat distorted or there is so very little of them that it is impossible to reconstruct the scenes depicted.

Nevertheless, it all works out to our advantage. The first and most important witnesses were generally the wealthiest and can be relied upon to have had better-made seals, which left clearer impressions. The very last of the witnesses may not even have had a chance to affix his signature, but we scarcely miss it. Of course, it doesn't always work out so that the impressions of the best seals are on the best part of the tablet. The most artistic impressions sometimes occur on the edges, where they are only imperfectly recorded, but taken all in all I am satisfied with the arrangement that the most important witnesses should "sign" first.

With the seal impressions on the tablet we have few of the disadvantages we should have in dealing with the seals themselves. We can date and give the exact origin of the tablet and hence of the seal impressions; for in most instances the complete date—year, month, and day—as well as the name of the city where the tablet was written are given at the bottom of the text. When we have only the seal, we can never tell whether it comes from the opposite corner of Mesopotamia or possibly even from some foreign land. Of course, sometimes the ancients themselves found or inherited and used for their own signatures seals of still earlier generations, but this can generally be detected when we have the seal impression and the accompanying text. For purposes of study the seal impression has another advantage over the seal. A modern forger cannot add his own mistakes on the impression of the seal which is found on the tablet, since no tablet can be changed so as to deceive an expert. We are therefore generally on safe ground here.

Business documents come to us in immense numbers from all parts of the land and from all periods of time. Each one of them, to be considered legal, had to be signed and therefore had to have at least one or two seal impressions. In the case of important transactions we have many more, sometimes as many as ten on a single tablet. Each little impression is a scene complete in itself, taken

A PASTORAL SCENE ON A SEAL IMPRESSION

from the daily life of the people. Sometimes as many as three or four personages are to be distinguished there, together with animals, temple utensils, altars, gods, furniture, musical instruments, and what not. We might therefore say that a well-preserved seal impression on a tablet will, for the purposes of art, be equivalent to a complete relief many yards long. From no land in antiquity have we ever recorded, or can we ever hope to record, one-thousandth part of the pictures which the seal impressions on clay tablets already in our possession give to us. Multiply what we have by the millions of documents still to be unearthed, and it is no exaggeration whatsoever to say that we gain a much better knowledge of comparative art for all periods and all parts of the land from the clay tablets than we ever can from any other source.

Chapter 16

ONE of the greatest discoveries ever made in Egypt at first aroused little interest among the people of the world. One day an Arab woman living in the little village of Tell el-Amarna came upon a large group of clay tablets. Such things were not expected in Egypt, but I am certain that the woman was not greatly excited by the discovery. Still, they were "antikas" and perhaps someone would want them. Before selling them, however, she and her friends decided to increase their number by cutting them in pieces. This job properly done, they offered the many fragments to the nearest dealers. The reception accorded by the dealers could not have been too hospitable either, but they knew a little more and were certainly aware that the tablets contained writing and therefore had a commercial value. Some enterprising merchant, consequently, offered a large group of them to one of the important museums in Europe. Scholars looked them over, but they were not quite convinced. Could Babylonian tablets come out of Egypt? Close study showed also some peculiarities in grammar and spelling. The lot was rejected as being the product of a modern forger.

After this experience the dealers began to sell the tablets to anyone who would buy, usually some unsuspecting tourist who wanted souvenirs. Sales were few, but the

TELL EL-AMARNA FROM THE AIR. DESERT AND TILLED LAND ARE SHARPLY DEFINED

merchants did not lose heart. They continued to offer their unpopular wares in various places. Finally the turning-point came when the Berlin Museum, to the ever-lasting credit of German scholarship, recognized the great importance of the tablets. The first lot was secured, and then began a frantic search for all the others. In this the German scholars were soon joined by all those who had at first refused to buy, and each now bought as many as he could. The net result is that the Amarna tablets are today scattered in many museums, one institution possessing a corner of a tablet and another perhaps the rest of it. The Americans, the last to enter the field of Assyriology, were farther away from the world's market and had to be content with remnants. For example, one tiny fragment, now known to be part of a larger piece in a European museum, was first studied in 1892 by a foreign scholar while it was in the hands of a dealer. Later this little fragment was acquired by an American missionary in Egypt and subsequently lost sight of by the scholarly world. Rediscovered among a number of Egyptian "antikas" which had been bought by the Art Institute of Chicago, it was generously presented to the Oriental Institute, where it is now highly prized.

But why were these tablets so important? The answer can be given in a few words. The documents, written

A FRAGMENT OF A BABYLONIAN TABLET FROM EGYPT—ONE OF THE FEW IN AMERICA

shortly after 1500 B.C., represent the official diplomatic correspondence between kings of Egypt and rulers of Palestine, Syria, Asia Minor, Babylonia, Assyria, and other places. It is the first complete diplomatic archive which has been discovered and, as can easily be imagined, throws an immense amount of light on the political condition of the times.

What we have learned about Asia Minor since these tablets were discovered has been a great surprise. According to history as we knew it, the Hittites had no business being important. They were occasionally mentioned in the Bible along with Jebusites, Amalekites, Perizzites, and so forth, and we had always thought they did not amount to much. The fact is that only small settlements of them lived in Palestine and came in contact with the Hebrews; their kingdom did extend at one time down into Syria, but it was really at home in Asia Minor. And one of the Amarna tablets is a letter from a Hittite ruler who was obviously on equal footing with the Egyptian pharaoh. Thus these tablets introduced us to the Hittites, who have since been rescued almost from oblivion and become the possessors of a mighty kingdom.

The Jebusites have also become more than a name. Jebus, we are told in the Bible, was the ancient name of Jerusalem; however that may be, a king of Jerusalem was carrying on a lively correspondence with the kings of Egypt at just about the time when the Hebrews were entering Canaan and taking possession of it. We thus have not only a thorough confirmation of a biblical fact but also the opinions of the side opposed to the incoming

204

AN EXCAVATOR IN MODERN TURKISH COSTUME BESIDE AN ANCIENT HITTITE SCULPTURE

Hebrews. The latter found in the land a civilization greatly superior to their own. That, however, did not seem to impress them to any extent, since the Canaanites were not the "chosen people of God." They therefore proceeded to wipe them out as well and as thoroughly as they could. The Canaanites, on the other hand, called these invaders "robbers" and "cutthroats" and decided to enlist help in driving them out of the land.

Canaan at this time was to some extent under the protection of Egypt. The king of Jerusalem therefore immediately dispatched a number of messengers to the pharaoh, asking him to send soldiers who could help. The pharaoh, Ikhnaton, was busy with a religious reformation, since he had determined to substitute the worship of one god for that of the many gods scattered throughout the land of Egypt. His reform brought on his head all sorts of troubles, and he had neither time nor desire to send troops to the king of Jerusalem. What he wrote him, if he wrote at all, we do not know, for in those times, apparently, they did not make copies of the letters sent, and all we have now are the letters delivered from outside. But whether he wrote or not, the fact remains that he did not send any troops. This we can easily find out by reading a second letter from the king of Jerusalem, reiterating the previous request and warning the pharaoh that unless he makes an effort to protect his domain, the land of Canaan will be lost to him. The second appeal found the same reception as the first, and in a last letter the king of Jerusalem tells him that soldiers are not needed any more; it is too late. Much of the land has already fallen into the hands of the invaders.

In reading the Bible, it is easy to see that the story of the conquest as given in the book of Joshua does not quite agree with that told in other books. While the former gives the impression that the conquest was purely military and that the land was thoroughly purged of its original inhabitants, from other books we gather the idea that the process was much slower and that the result was obtained in a somewhat roundabout way. The Amarna tablets tell us just how this was accomplished, and in them we can see the invaders allying themselves with many powerful native princes. The system of alliances was probably quite effective in obtaining the desired result of subjugating the people, but it also gave a great deal of trouble to the invaders. That part of the population which was permitted to go free and to live in peace began to influence the less cultured invaders to a very large extent. The whole religious history of the Hebrews is a constant fight against the Baal worshipers, who not only continued in their old ways but many times practically succeeded in luring the invaders away from their God, Jehovah, and converting them to Baal.

The correspondence with the kings of Babylonia is very interesting. To be sure, Babylonia at that time was under a foreign dynasty which governed the land weakly in a period of political chaos. These Babylonian kings kept writing to the pharaohs for gold, a metal not found in Mesopotamia or very near to it. Egypt, with mines in Sinai and in Nubia, was probably the best source, and the Babylonians sent as many presents as they could and begged to have gold in exchange: "In your land gold is plentiful as the dust of the earth." The Egyptians didn't see it that way and at least from the Babylonian standpoint were rather stingy in sending the precious metal. It must be said to the credit of the Babylonian rulers that regardless of economic decay in their own land they did not want to go off the gold standard. In spite of all discouragements they held on.

AN EGYPTIAN IN BABYLONIA DREW THIS
FIGURE ON A STAMPED BRICK

Other letters from Babylonian sovereigns tell of two princesses from Babylon who were sent to pharaohs as wives. Imagine what must have been the feelings of those poor girls! They were being transported to the other end of the then known world to become the brides of men whom they had never seen before and who were different from them not only in civilization but even in race. But then, as now, princesses of the blood royal had very little to say about their husbands; the interests of diplomacy had to be considered first of all.

Some day, if we are fortunate, we are going to round out the Tell el-Amarna archives by finding the letters written by the Egyptian pharaohs in answer to those they so carefully kept. It will take time because these were scattered all over the ancient world. Also, I am quite certain, some of them are lost forever. But there is already a beginning. It is of interest to know that a treaty with a king of the Hittites, the text of which had been found in Egyptian hieroglyphics, has also been found in Asia Minor, nicely written in Babylonian on a clay tablet. Since Babylonian was the official language of diplomacy, it is certain that the one written on clay was considered the authoritative text, the Egyptian being merely the translation of it. We know how troublesome it is today to translate important official documents, in order to render as closely as possible the same meaning in different languages. But since there is always a possibility of disagreement, one of the versions must be the standard. The old translators probably had the same troubles as modern ones.

At this point it might be asked, "Why should the

Babylonian 'letters' be the official ones? Did not the Egyptians have a very high degree of civilization and could not Egyptian have been used as the language of diplomacy?" A language is imposed either through military or through cultural conquest. While Babylonian conquerors from about 2500 B.C. on had succeeded in extending their authority throughout an immense area, still these military conquests were only intermittent. Now and then a king would go out and plant the standards of his gods in regions inhabited by "barbarians," but such triumphs came only under the leadership of great monarchs, and the influence on the development of civilization must have been slight. There never was a great Babylonian empire that endured for a very long period of time. Therefore, the conquest which brought about the adoption of Babylonian as the language of diplomacy was a purely cultural one.

Moreover, while Egypt was a remote country, surrounded by deserts, seas, and backward peoples, Mesopotamia was in the very middle of a great cultural area. Dealings with other lands were carried on at all times. Perhaps nowhere else, with the exception of Egypt, had an independent system of writing been developed. No wonder, then, that just as the more backward peoples of Europe took up the Latin alphabet and adopted it for their languages, so all the peoples surrounding Babylonia and Assyria adopted for their own languages the Babylonian method of writing. Just as Latin in the Middle Ages was the common language of scholars, so Babylonian became the common language of culture and diplomacy. Babylonian scribes took their styluses and proceeded to teach all the people around them the art of cuneiform writing. They prepared dictionaries in which words of the local language were written down phonetically side by side with the corresponding words in Semitic Babylonian. Together with their styluses, they carried also their knowledge; and just as the great literary masterpieces were used as textbooks for teaching writing in the schools of Babylonia, so these same classics were the books from which the barbarians first learned reading and spelling. Of course, we don't at all class the Egyptians among barbarians, for they had an advanced civilization of their own, but since they could not teach their language to the whole world, they had to do the best they could and use, in their dealings with outsiders, the language that the outsiders knew best.

Thus we have the Egyptian scribe pondering over this strange system of writing, and some of the Amarna tablets are marked with red ink, indicating the places where he had decided that one word ended and the next began. In the scribe's study of this foreign language he, like the Babylonian scribe, turned to the Babylonian legends, and this is why among the Amarna tablets was also found a fragment of one of the most common and most beautiful of the Babylonian stories. The profound significance of this can be grasped only if we try to determine what influence Babylonian writing and culture might have had on the surrounding nations—in my opinion, much greater than is at present suspected.

Chapter 17

A GENERATION ago, natives working on a mound near the ancient city of Caesarea in Turkey began to find baked clay tablets which eventually came into the hands of dealers and were sold through the world's markets. After some years an Assyriologist went to the place and found a good many more. These tablets, and others like them which have since been found at various places in Turkey, have been called "Cappadocian." But their discovery immediately raised all sorts of disturbing problems. They were all business documents and letters, except for a fragment of a law—the presence of which can very easily be understood, since business must be transacted according to law. But there were no literary texts, no psalms or incantations, no learned treatises of any kind—only business. From internal evidence the tablets could be dated about 2000 B.C. They clearly belonged to a large group of Assyrian merchants who had settled in that part of Asia Minor and had acted as agents for other Assyrians in a different part of the world. That this group was not the only one is proved by correspondence carried on by these merchants with men in different cities. That they were in constant contact also with the mother-country is evident from the fact that they still referred to the city Ashur as "the city" par excellence, as *urbs* was used in later times for Rome.

Now the question arises: How could these Assyrians be there at a time when, to the best of our knowledge, Assyria as a powerful nation did not yet exist? That is, how could they safely establish themselves in a foreign country in such large numbers unless they had the protection of their own country? Must we think of a great Assyrian empire dating as far back as 2000 B.C.? If so, why have we not heard of it? Of course, I must mention here that the archeologist's work in Mesopotamia has only begun and that, in spite of the hundreds of thousands of documents already uncovered, we have only the crumbs which have fallen from the table. An argument from silence under the circumstances doesn't go very far. But still, we should have heard about it. Further, these Assyrians were

A BUSINESS MAN'S RECORDS—CAPPADOCIAN TABLETS AS DISCOVERED

peaceful merchants, and, stranger still, the language they used is perfectly pure—we might say the purest that has ever been found—and there was nothing crude about these early colonists. How does this fit into the common picture of Assyrians as uncouth soldiers who made their living preying upon defenseless neighbors? We know this to be altogether wrong in so far as it applies to later Assyrian times, but still, going back to 2000 B.C., we might expect them to be little rough, at least in the beginning of their history. And what was the relationship between these Assyrian colonists and the local people of Asia Minor? We know about their trade, but we don't know about the cultural relationships which must have followed the traders. Did local princes learn how to use the Akkadian language and employ it in dealings among themselves? Shall we consider all the Assyrian documents found in several places in Asia Minor as originating from Assyrian colonists? Or are some of them entirely local products, and were the Assyrians responsible only for having taught the local people how to write in the Assyrian language? Many of these problems cannot be solved at present, or can be solved only in part, and so we shall let them go.

But Asia Minor later on gave us a much greater surprise than the discovery of the business archives of Assyrian colonists. From the first excavation conducted at Boghazköy, a place not far from the present capital of the Turkish nation, there came a large number of documents, about ten thousand. This time they are written almost entirely in the local languages. The bulk of them can be dated roughly between 1500 and 1200 B.C., and

214

THE REMAINS OF A FORTRESS IN ASIA MINOR

this is exactly as it should be. If people who do not know how to write come in contact with more civilized ones among whom writing is common, they borrow not only the system of writing but also the language, for at first the two are closely associated. Later on an enterprising individual will discover that it is not necessary to use a foreign language but that the system of writing can be adapted to the local language. Thus the second step will be: same system, different language. The third and final step, when it is taken, is to modify the system so as to make it more suitable for the language; and so, ultimately, we have a new and simplified way of writing the local language.

By 2000 B.C. the native population of Asia Minor had become acquainted with the cuneiform way of writing through the Assyrian colonists; but, since it was used only for business purposes, it never had any great popularity. A few hundred years later, people in the same locality again came into contact with Babylonia, but this time with its literary productions. Adequately impressed, they adopted the system of writing and adapted it to their own language—in other words, the second step of the development outlined above had been taken by 1400 B.C.

Finding at Boghazköy the cuneiform script used for writing more than one language was not the most striking discovery made there. One of these languages, called Hittite, is basically an Indo-European language not far removed from ancient Greek. In fact, a scholar of my acquaintance insists that the language is really Greek and that the differences are due simply to the fact that it is a great deal older than the Greek we know. He may find it difficult to establish his thesis, but the similarity is certainly there. Incidentally, this is the first time for the Indo-Europeans, the so-called fathers of civilization, to score a point—now that the myth of the great antiquity of the Indian books has been completely exploded by modern scholars—and to stand revealed in history as the creators of really old documents.

We shall not enter here into a detailed description of the different languages; suffice it to say that, besides the Indo-European language which we call Hittite, there are at least five other distinct languages, with Indian or Iranian words scattered throughout. Among this number we do not even count the ancient Sumerian and Babylonian, which of course had to be found there. In fact, from Boghazköy we have so-called "syllabaries" which are really dictionaries. In one column the ancient sign is reproduced, in parallel columns its Sumerian, Akkadian, and Hittite equivalents.

As elsewhere, the ancient epics come in for their share of attention in the documents found, and we have fragments of the Gilgamesh epic translated into Hittite and Hurrian. Omen texts have been discovered here which very closely resemble the Akkadian ones, and sometimes we have them in bilingual redactions, Akkadian and Hittite. Especially striking are the astronomical omens, which predict the future from movements of the stars and planets and which are very like those from Assyria. As in Babylonia, predictions were commonly based on an examination of the liver of a slaughtered sheep; inscribed liver models similar to those from Mesopotamia suggest the origin of the practice, and a parallel model in faraway Italian Etruria represents another station in the journey of one phase of Babylonian culture.

Most of the texts come from the royal archives. What they can tell us about the religious cults and temple services, therefore, will be largely the practices of officialdom. But there is a surprisingly large number of well-preserved rituals telling what the various classes of officials and public servants should and should not do. The offerings to be brought to the temple, the daily care of the gods, the particular rituals for the celebration of multitudinous feasts and feast days—all are minutely described. Occasionally and incidentally we secure a

217

glimpse of the home religion, as when we read the ritual to be performed if an accident disturbs the regular procedure of birth.

On the political side we have references to the great king Sargon of Akkad and to one of his successors, Naram-Sin, who lived long ago in the third millennium B.C. Here, too, we have what may be called the first constitution to be found anywhere. Established by the king Telepinus, it lays down the rules for royal succession, the rights of the people and of the noblemen. It limits the power of the king, whose authority evidently was originally absolute. This constitution is preceded by a long preamble summarizing preceding history. This same history is, of course, supplemented by the regular historical inscriptions and the kings' annals, and there are also several treaties, the most famous being the one between the Egyptian pharaoh and the Hittite king, mentioned in the preceding chapter. We have already noted the fact that a portion of the Hittite law code has been discovered.

Too interesting to be omitted is a manual for the care of horses. It tells how to train them, how much exercise they should be given, how much rest, and so on. I believe this to be the very first manual on such a subject ever found.

But besides their intrinsic importance, the Cappadocian tablets and the Boghazköy archives help us trace one of the main highways along which civilization marched in its spread throughout the world. I say "one of the main highways," because naturally intercourse between nations does not follow any single route. Civilization will pass from one people to another in a series of

LIVER MODELS FROM
BABYLONIA (*top*), ASIA
MINOR (*center*), AND
ETRUSCAN ITALY (*bottom*)

currents that sometimes cannot even be traced, but here we have Asia Minor strongly under Assyrian influence as far back as 2000 B.C., if not earlier. Out of this developed the great local civilizations which were nurtured from the very beginning on Babylonian science. Asia Minor was just across the sea from Greece; in fact, from the earliest times the Greeks had colonized most of the coast nearest them. Could these early settlers have been absolutely unresponsive to the influences surrounding them? If they were, then they were at such a low stage of civilization that they cannot have contributed much of their own. And would these colonists start inventing scientific theories about the origin of the world, when all this development was at their disposal and carried with it the prestige of hoary antiquity?

A priori we must think that the great contribution Greece gave to the world was not in the main original. The Greeks took what they found, adapted it to their own needs, and carried it on to still greater perfection. It is idle at present to meditate about Sumerian influence on Greek myths and legends and on the speculations of ancient Greek philosophers. Resemblances can already be traced, but the safest thing to do before attempting comparisons is to wait and first piece together and translate the Sumerian texts. There is no doubt whatsoever in my mind that, when such a study is possible, we shall be astonished by its results.

Besides dependence in philosophical and religious ideas, we shall find a background for ancient Greek art. It is interesting to know that a very common representation in the art of the early Greek world, a goat on either side of the "Tree of Life," is a very ancient oriental symbol that goes back as far as we can trace and is frequently found on the seal impressions on the documents from Nuzi. But it is useless to speculate. Suffice it for the present to say that we shall have to abandon most of our old ideas and completely re-write the earliest chapters of Greek history in the light of the new information which is constantly being given by the clay tablets.

THE "TREE OF LIFE" MOTIF IN THE IMPRESSION OF AN OLD
BABYLONIAN CYLINDER SEAL

Chapter 18

W E KNEW from the very beginning of Babylonian decipherment that cuneiform writing
had been adapted to languages foreign to
Babylonia. In fact, the key to decipherment was given,
as will be remembered, by the trilingual inscriptions
found in Persia. There by the side of the Babylonian we
had the Elamite inscriptions, which used a smaller number of signs than the Babylonian but were still syllabic
in character. By the side of Elamite we had also Old
Persian, in which the cuneiform signs had been reduced
almost to a regular alphabet. Whether this change was
effected independently or whether it was suggested by
the already circulating Semitic alphabets is impossible to
say, though probably the second alternative is the right
one. The Boghazköy archives had also confirmed the fact
that cuneiform characters could be adapted for many
different languages. Other evidence for this had likewise
been discovered even in the mountains of Armenia, where
the old kings had given us inscriptions both in Assyrian
and in their own language. We were, therefore, quite
well prepared for a number of surprises, but hardly ready
for the epoch-making discoveries that have been made at
Ras Shamra.

Ras Shamra is the modern name for a little place of
no present importance in Syria. Syria and Palestine, as

everyone knows, formed a sort of bridge uniting the great civilizations of Egypt and Mesopotamia. Traders were constantly passing through these countries, and the lands changed hands a number of times at different periods of their history. For many years a large Egyptian trading post had been established in the ancient city of Byblos in Syria, and other reminders of Egypt have been found at several sites, especially in the northern part. A few inscribed clay tablets have also been discovered in scattered places both in Syria and in Palestine, testifying to constant Babylonian influence. Hittites had likewise made their presence felt, and Hittite monuments have been found, again particularly in the northern part of the area. Here was a country well known to have been subjected

THIS COLUMN BASE ON THE PORCH OF A SYRIAN PALACE BETRAYS HITTITE CULTURAL INFLUENCE

to many influences from surrounding lands, but as yet little had appeared which originated with the local population.

Just a few years ago a native passing by a low mound near Ras Shamra noticed the remains of what appeared to be a tomb. The government immediately became interested, not only in the objects within this tomb, but also in the mound of Ras Shamra itself, from which had already come a number of cylinder seals. One of these seals even bore a cuneiform inscription. A scientific expedition at once began to dig in the place, and results were obtained immediately, for over forty of the everlasting clay tablets rewarded the excavators in their first season. Since then, the actual number of documents found has not been made public, and in fact it would be useless to do so since excavations are continuing and the number is constantly increasing, but scholars have already published the first results.

Again among the tablets come documents written in Sumerian and Akkadian, as a sort of official stamp that at the bottom of the local development stands once more the civilization of Mesopotamia. We should not have needed that, since clay tablets in themselves, especially in a land where other kinds of writing material are plentiful, would have been sufficient proof. It is still impossible to date the finds accurately, though perhaps 1400 B.C. is sufficiently close for the group. Some of the texts written in Babylonian may prove to be older if we follow the usual process of culture transmission: first, system of writing and language; second, same system and different language; third, new system and new language.

The real surprise at Ras Shamra was, however, this: The people living there had adapted the old cuneiform signs—or new ones invented by them—to an alphabet with which they wrote inscriptions in two different languages. One was certainly an early dialect of Phoenician, the other a language which closely resembles Hurrian—spoken by the "Horites" of the Bible. Since the discovery is so recent, scholars have devoted most of their attention so far to the Phoenician, which is far easier to translate, as the language belongs to the well-known Semitic group. In fact, it took no time at all to find out the values of the groups of wedges that stood for the letters of the alphabet. The most difficult texts can now be read with a sufficient degree of confidence.

And so we now have ancient Phoenicians telling their own tales—and they do seem to like to tell them, for a large number of long myths and epics have been found in the group. Bible students from now on will have to take into consideration not only the influences coming from Babylonia and Egypt but also those from contemporaneous Phoenicians. Since we knew from the very beginning that the people in Canaan had played a large part in the development of Hebrew religion, it is gratifying to hear them contribute whatever they know.

As has been said before, most of the texts studied so far are written in the Phoenician language. The other language is so difficult that it has had little chance to tell us what it knows. But still its very presence in an alphabetic form at that early age raises a number of bewildering problems. Which one of the two languages first developed the alphabet? Did the Hurrians start, and the

SINAITIC	CANAANITE-PHOENICIAN	EARLY GREEK	LATER GREEK	LATIN	ENGLISH
		Λ	Λ	A	A
		B	B	B	B
		٦	٢	C G	C,G
		Δ	Δ	D	D
		٦	E	E	E
	Y	Y	Y	F V	F,U,V, W,Y
(?)		I	I		Z
	H H	B	B	H	H
	⊗	⊗	⊗		(Th)
	Z	٤	٤	I	I,J
		∤	K		K
		V⌐L	L ⌃	L	L
		٣	⌐	M	M
		V	N	N	N
		⊞	⊞	X	(X)
	○○	○	○	O	O
		٦	Γ	P	P
		Μ	M		(S)
	φφφ	Φ	φ	Q	Q
	٩	٩	P	R	R
	W	٤	٤	S	S
	×	T	T	T	T

A TABLE SHOWING THE ORIGIN OF OUR ALPHABET

Phoenicians follow, or did the development go the opposite way? Is there a connection between this alphabet, used for Phoenician and Hurrian, and another alphabet discovered on the Sinai peninsula not very long ago? Or must we revise all our ideas concerning the purveyance and transmission of the alphabet which we thought the Sinaitic inscriptions had settled once and for all? The more we increase our knowledge, the more we increase our worries. Who knows but that tomorrow, after we have readjusted ourselves to the many surprises caused by the discoveries at Ras Shamra, a new group of tablets from some other part of the old world may appear and upset our ideas again! But eventually, out of the uncertainties and vain gropings, the truth is sure to be obtained.

How far into Asia can the knowledge and use of clay tablets and cuneiform characters have penetrated, and how many of the lost civilizations can we expect to come to light again? A definite answer is impossible now, but already there are signs marking the road we should follow if we are to discover an answer in the years to come. The Elamite texts which played a part in the decipherment of all cuneiform were only the last descendants of a long line of earlier Elamite inscriptions written in cuneiform characters on clay. The use of this medium for the language is attested as early as 3000 B.C., and subsequent inscriptions tell of Elamite kingdoms down through the centuries. Though most of our information about them comes from southwestern Iran, we have also discovered that people in the central part of the plateau also knew how to use the reed stylus of the scribe.

From some localities of India, during the last few years, have come very early seals with representations of animals and a kind of pictographic writing. Valiant but fruitless have been the attempts to decipher what is so clearly written on the seals, and what five thousand years ago was, no doubt, read by schoolboys. However, excavations in early strata in Mesopotamia have produced

EVIDENCE OF INDIAN (*top*) AND BABYLONIAN (*bottom*) CULTURAL LINKS

other seals of exactly the same type. Obviously there were commercial relations between Mesopotamia and parts of India in the third millennium B.C., or perhaps even earlier.

Encouraged by the finding of these seals, the English government participated in the work, and ten years of excavations in India have added two thousand years to the history of the land. Complete cities have been unearthed, and the objects discovered there bear witness to a very high degree of civilization. Unfortunately, all the cities are too old and antedate the discovery, or at least the use, of writing, and our ever helpful clay tablets have not been found. But, if writing was known in India in the first part of the third millennium, it is reasonable to believe that it wasn't forgotten afterward. Commercial relations between India and Mesopotamia were intensified with the passing centuries, and even if the Indians did not succeed in developing a system of writing of their own, they always had access to that of the Babylonians. It is therefore much more than probable, we might say certain, that some day in the right place the Indian documents will be found.

Here it is worth while to touch upon a question: What language will they be in, and what will be their content? As is well known, the indigenous population of India was conquered in early times, perhaps about 1200 B.C., by the so-called Indo-Europeans. The conquerors treated the local peoples very cruelly, made slaves of them, and laid upon them all manner of restrictions. In other words, the original population became the pariahs, or the untouchables, of today. If we ever do get clay tablets from India, I am sure that the very first ones will describe for us the civilization of the untouchables and will prove it to be much higher and more fully developed than that of their conquerors. The tables will be turned, and the poor pariahs will have something to boast about. Who knows? This might even help in breaking up the terrible caste system.

It is impossible even to guess how far east Babylonian tablets may have crept, and to what distance overland the Babylonian system of writing wandered. Some scholars have tried to prove that Chinese picture-writing had a common origin with the picture-writing of the ancient Sumerians, that the two systems followed independent lines of development, and that while the Babylonians soon abandoned, in large part, ideographic for phonetic writing, the Chinese stuck to the old system. But all this is pure speculation and is extremely unlikely. We are still ignorant of the real facts, and so we shall remain until lands far distant from Mesopotamia have been more thoroughly explored for the express purpose of revealing these facts.

Epilogue

In this book we have touched on only a few of the many phases of life that have been revealed to us by the clay tablets—diaries of the human past. In closing, we may say this: Whereas up to a few years ago, man's life before the Christian Era belonged mostly to the realm of mystery, myth, and legend, it has now through the apparently dull, lifeless, and unintelligible inscriptions been brought out into the light to such an extent that, so far as some phases of human activity are concerned, the "dark ages" are those which are nearest to us! In spite of the immense wealth of Latin and Greek literature, we do not know nearly so much about certain aspects of the daily life in Greece and Rome as we know about similar phases of life in a little corner of the Mesopotamian plain. This state of affairs is sure to continue, and with further discovery and study of clay documents ancient oriental history will be enriched with source material that in the wealth of its details bearing on public and private life yields to none.

Suppose our modern civilization should go to pieces—and the supposition is not a far-fetched one, considering the absolute idiocy which is controlling international relations. We are like children who have been given some deadly weapons and who do not have sense enough to know how those weapons should be used. Let us suppose, therefore, that another great world-war should start fifty or a hundred years from now. The horrors of the last one cannot compare with what civilized mankind will be able to do with the help of science. Gas and bacteria warfare might play havoc with both conqueror and conquered. Suppose further that the bacteria, even after the war was over, should continue their work. Whatever we have accomplished throughout several millenniums might face destruction. Yet mankind would not be completely wiped out. Some of the backward races, by the very fact that they were backward, would not have been able to participate effectively in the world's struggle and would be saved. Let us suppose again that man once more begins his ascent and that archeologists of ten thousand years hence begin to piece together whatever data they may find about the history and civilization of the nations that have preceded them. What will these archeologists find in the ruins of a great American city?

Assuredly, they will discover the immense skeletons of our skyscrapers. They will be able to study the plans of the buildings and will be duly impressed by the architectural achievements of the peoples of today. They will discover the intricate network of subways and may conclude from them that while the ruling class of America liked to live high up in the air, probably the slaves were kept in underground dwellings. They will find most of our pottery and our glass. The gold objects and coins will always be there, and some of our machinery will remain as an additional proof of our mechanical development.

But what about our achievements in other lines? All our books and writings will have disintegrated. The excavators may find an inscription chiseled on the cornerstone of a building or on the pedestal of a statue. If they work very carefully they may be able to find the signs indicating the names of the streets. I said "if they work very carefully" because by that time the iron backing will have gone completely, and all they will have will be a thin film of enamel that will drop to pieces unless very carefully handled. Here and there they will probably find some other inscriptions on metals or coins of imperishable material. But the real achievements of our civilization will be lost forever. Perhaps the archeologists of those times will come to the conclusion that we were even more materialistic than we really are, and the judgment they will pass on us may not be very favorable.

At the same time, in the course of their investigations, archeologists will go again and excavate again in the lands of the Near East. All those Babylonian tablets that we shall have left undug —99 per cent of the total—will still be waiting in their graves to tell their messages. And they will tell them all over again; their ancient history and the ancient civilizations will be pieced together again by scholars of tomorrow, who will probably decide that the "golden age" of mankind was in the second and third millenniums B.C., after which barbarians took command and messed things up so thoroughly with their machines and mechanical inventions that they finally brought their civilization to crash on their own heads!

Acknowledgments

TO THE many people who have assisted in the publication of *They Wrote on Clay*, this brief note is dedicated. For their invaluable assistance in editing the manuscript, I am most grateful to Professors A. T. Olmstead and W. F. Geers, to Drs. W. H. Dubberstein, R. M. Engberg, and I. J. Gelb, and to Mrs. Erna S. Hallock, Miss Doris R. Fessler, and my wife, Frances T. Cameron. Especial appreciation is accorded the University of Chicago Press, in particular Professor Gordon J. Laing, Miss Mary D. Alexander, and Mr. Herman J. Bauman.

To the Oriental Institute and its Director, Professor John A. Wilson, I am indebted for permission to use illustrations from the Institute files—the great majority of those which appear. Due acknowledgment must also be made for the illustrations on the pages here listed and published through the courtesy of the following: page 44: R.A.F. Official-Crown Copyright Reserved; pages 3, 14, and 183: the Joint Expedition of the British Museum and the University Museum (University of Pennsylvania) to Ur; pages 27 (redrawn by W. R. Romig), 102, 162, 173, and 219 (top): the Trustees of the British Museum; page 87 (top): the Museum of Science and Industry, Chicago; page 100: the Berlin Museum; page 59: the Deutsche Forschungsgemeinschaft; pages 126 and 219 (center): the Deutsche Orient-Gesellschaft; page 62 (drawn by Professor A. Poebel): Ginn and Company; pages 46, 53, and 202: James H. Breasted, Jr.; page 70: Dr. E. R. Lacheman; page 226 (columns 1 and 2): Professor M. Sprengling (redrawn by W. R. Romig); page 208: Mr. Sidney Smith and the Baghdad Museum; page 15: the *Illustrated London News;* page 84: De Morgan, *Mémoires de la déléga-*

234

tion en Perse, I; page 149: De Sarzec, *Découvertes en Chaldée*, II; page 153: Pottier, *Les Antiquités assyriennes;* page 167: André Parrot, *Mari, une ville perdue;* pages 160–61: C. S. Fisher, *Excavations at Nippur;* pages 36, 37, 69, 81, 87 (bottom), 97, 113, 179, 180, 182, 185, 188, and 189: Mrs. Edward Chiera.

GEORGE G. CAMERON

PHOENIX BOOKS
in Sociology

P 7   *Louis Wirth:* The Ghetto

P 10   *Edwin H. Sutherland,* EDITOR: The Professional Thief, by a professional thief

P 24   *B. A. Botkin,* EDITOR: Lay My Burden Down: A Folk History of Slavery

P 28   *David M. Potter:* People of Plenty: Economic Abundance and the American Character

P 71   *Nels Anderson:* The Hobo: The Sociology of the Homeless Man

P 82   *W. Lloyd Warner:* American Life: Dream and Reality

P 92   *Joachim Wach:* Sociology of Religion

P 117 *Herbert A. Thelen:* Dynamics of Groups at Work

P 124 *Margaret Mead and Martha Wolfenstein,* EDITORS: Childhood in Contemporary Cultures

P 129 *John P. Dean and Alex Rosen:* A Manual of Intergroup Relations

P 138 *Frederic M. Thrasher:* The Gang: A Study of 1,313 Gangs in Chicago (Abridged)

P 162 *Thomas F. O'Dea:* The Mormons

P 170 *Anselm Strauss,* EDITOR: George Herbert Mead on Social Psychology

P 171 *Otis Dudley Duncan,* EDITOR: William F. Ogburn on Culture and Social Change

P 172 *Albert J. Reiss, Jr.,* EDITOR: Louis Wirth on Cities and Social Life

P 174 *Morris Janowitz:* The Military in the Political Development of New Nations

P 183 *Robert E. L. Faris and H. Warren Dunham:* Mental Disorders in Urban Areas

P 204 *Allison Davis and Burleigh and Mary Gardner:* Deep South (Abridged)

P 205 *E. Franklin Frazier:* The Negro Family in the United States

P 214 *Charles S. Johnson:* Shadow of the Plantation

P 219 *Eileen Younghusband,* EDITOR: Casework with Families and Children

P 226 *Harry Elmer Barnes,* EDITOR: An Introduction to the History of Sociology (Abridged)

P 242 *Morris Janowitz,* EDITOR: W. I. Thomas on Social Organization and Social Personality

P 244 *Bernard R. Berelson et al.:* Voting

P 245 *Harold F. Gosnell:* Negro Politicians

P 253 *Ernest W. Burgess and Donald J. Bogue,* EDITORS: Urban Sociology

P 262 *Manning Nash:* Machine Age Maya

P 263 *Morris Janowitz:* The Community Press in an Urban Setting

P 271 *Robert Blauner:* Alienation and Freedom

P 272 *George H. Mead:* Mind, Self, and Society

P 274 *Louis Schneider,* EDITOR: The Scottish Moralists on Human Nature and Society

P 275 *Ralph H. Turner,* EDITOR: Robert E. Park on Social Control and Collective Behavior